An MT-Oriented Study of Corresponding Lexical Chunks in Business Correspondences from English to Chinese

Fumao Hu

An MT-Oriented Study of Corresponding Lexical Chunks in Business Correspondences from English to Chinese

Science Press
Beijing

Springer

Fumao Hu
Luoyang Institute of Science
and Technology
Luoyang, Henan, China

Translated by
Jing An
Beijing International Studies University
Beijing, Beijing Shi, China

ISBN 978-981-99-4976-2 ISBN 978-981-99-4977-9 (eBook)
https://doi.org/10.1007/978-981-99-4977-9

Jointly published with Science Press
The print edition is not for sale in China (Mainland). Customers from China (Mainland) please order the print book from: Science Press.
ISBN of the Co-Publisher's edition: 978-7-03-056061-2

Translation from the Chinese language edition: "An MT-Oriented Study of Corresponding Lexical Chunks in Business Correspondences from English to Chinese" by Fumao Hu, © Science Press 2018. Published by Science Press. All Rights Reserved.

This Springer imprint is published by the registered company Springer Nature Singapore Pte Ltd.
The registered company address is: 152 Beach Road, #21-01/04 Gateway East, Singapore 189721, Singapore

Contents

Chapter 1
Related Studies on Formulaic Sequences

1.1 Introduction

On May 16–17, 2009, the First National Symposium on Formulaic Sequence Teaching and Research was held at the School of International Studies of the University of International Business and Economics, with the theme of "Formulaic Sequences from Multidimensional Perspectives". Proceedings of this seminar were collected in *Advances in Theoretical and Empirical Research on Formulaic Language* which was published in December, 2012. In the preface, the editor points out that the study of formulaic sequences in China is in its infancy stage, and there are still many problems to be solved. It is suggested that the study should focus on the following aspects: (1) the definition of formulaic sequences; (2) theoretical research on formulaic sequences; (3) comparative study of formulaic sequences in English and Chinese; (4) empirical research on formulaic sequence; (5) the relationship between formulaic sequences and constructions (Wang & Chen, 2012).

In this chapter, through combing domestic and foreign literature, we analyze and review the current status of research on formulaic sequences from three aspects: theoretical research on formulaic sequences and construction grammar, research on formulaic sequences in machine translation, and research on formulaic sequences for business letters, in order to pave the way for exploring the theoretical model of formulaic sequences composition analysis and the definition of formulaic sequences for business letters in machine translation.

F. Hu, *An MT-Oriented Study of Corresponding Lexical Chunks in Business Correspondences from English to Chinese*,
https://doi.org/10.1007/978-981-99-4977-9_1

1.2 Theoretical Research on Formulaic Sequences and Construction Grammar

Formulaic sequences originated from psychological studies. In the 1950s, American psychologists G. A. Miller and J. A. Selfridge proposed the idea of "chunking", stating that individual pieces of information are bound together into a whole in processing memory information, and short-term memory could only hold "7 ± 2" chunks of information. In 1975, linguist Becker first introduced the concept of "prefabricated chunks", special lexical phrases in English. Becker defines lexical chunks as a particular multiword phenomenon and presented in the form of formulaic fixed and semi-fixed chunks. According to Becker, lexical chunk, is the smallest unit of human communication. Later on, chunks have received widespread attention from all over the world. Bolinger (1975) argues that there are an incredible number of chunks in human language. Krashen and Scarcella (1978) consider chunks as "semi-fixed pattern" between the traditional free combination of words and fixed idioms. Fillmore et al. (1979) emphasizes that prefabricated language can help language learners establish and internalize the grammatical rules of the target language. Pawley and Syder (1983) emphasize the need for second language learners to acquire a large number of chunks to solve the problem of authenticity and fluency in language acquisition. Peters (1983) sees chunks as formulaic frameworks which are analyzable. Renouf and Sinclair (1991) point out that chunks are strings of words that occur with high frequency and varying degrees of lexicalization, constituting the basic linguistic units of English. Nattinger and DeCarrico (1992) define chunks as linguistic structures of varying length between traditional lexical and syntactic structures. Compared with ad hoc assembled phrases, lexical phrases have a more fixed form, function, and idiomatic meaning. Ellis (1996) holds the view that chunks are usually stored or extracted as a whole as a structural unit in mental lexicon. According to Lewis (1997), there are a wealth of fixed or semi-fixed linguistic structures with both syntactic and lexical features between the lexical and syntactic levels. Altenberg (1998) states that up to 80% of natural English discourse is composed of various formulaic structures, and the chunk is the basic linguistic units of English. Biber et al. (1999) distinguish multi-word units in terms of idiomatic, collocational, and lexico-grammatical relations, and on this basis propose the concept of lexical bundles. Widdowson (1999) argues that language consists of two parts, comprehensive, memorized chunks and analytic grammatical rules. Schmitt (2000) sees chunks as linguistic structures in which multi-word units of different lengths (including compounds, phrases, idioms, etc.) have both lexical and grammatical features with specific discourse functions. Wray (2002) expounds that chunk are strings of prefabricated coherent or incoherent words or other units of meaning that are stored in memory as a whole and are extracted directly when used without grammatical generation or analysis. Her definition is well accepted in the academic circle, and most scholars in China have adopted her definition.

However, due to the different research backgrounds, purposes, perspectives and methodology, the academic world has different opinions on chunks, such as on its naming. Scholars use different terms for chunks, for example, "prefabricated routines and patterns" by Brown (1973), "idiosyncratic chunks" by Becker (1975), "formulaic utterances" by Wong-Fillmore (1976), "gambits" by Keller (1979), "formulaic speech" by Ellis (1985), "Chunks" by Nattinger (1988), "prefabricated chunks" by Widdowson (1989), "lexical phrases" by Nattinger and DeCarrico (1992), "ready-made complex units" by Cowie (1998), "lexical chunks/items" by Lewis (1993), "lexical patterns" by Hunston and Francis (1999), "formulaic sequences" by Wray (2000), "multi-word items" by Moon (1997), "phraseology" by Stubbs (2002), "cluster" by Scott (2004), "lexical bundle" by Cortes (2004), "formulaic expression" by Lancker-Sidtis and Rallon (2004), etc. Wray (2002) points out that there are more than 50 terms describing this phenomenon, but the core of the discussion is in fact the greater or lesser part of a phenomenon that is essentially the same.

Foreign research on formulaic sequences is mainly from three perspectives: first, language acquisition and second language teaching, which involves research on the definition of the linguistic phenomenon referred to by formulaic sequences and its importance, the advantages of teaching formulaic sequences and its application in second language acquisition, and the empirical studies about these contents. Second, psycholinguistics, which mainly focuses on whether learners regard them as formulaic sequences and whether they are stored and extracted as a whole. Third, corpus linguistics, in which formulaic sequences are identified and defined based on frequency of occurrence in the corpus. Based on frequency and common sense, it is possible to determine which are formulaic sequences and which are conventions retained and remembered as a whole by a certain language group, although high frequency is not always a reasonable factor. Generally, these three perspectives and methods complement each other (Wang & Qian, 2009).

Since the 1980s, some domestic scholars have also shown a strong interest in the research about chunks, as shown in Figs. 1.1 and 1.2.

As of January 1, 2014, the author conducted a search for the precise keyword "formulaic sequences" of papers published in CNKI. The results showed that 2,216 articles were found, among which the first paper that mentioned formulaic sequences was published in 1985. From 1987 to 1999, there were only 13 relevant papers and the number gradually increased from 2000 to 2009, with a total of 721 during this

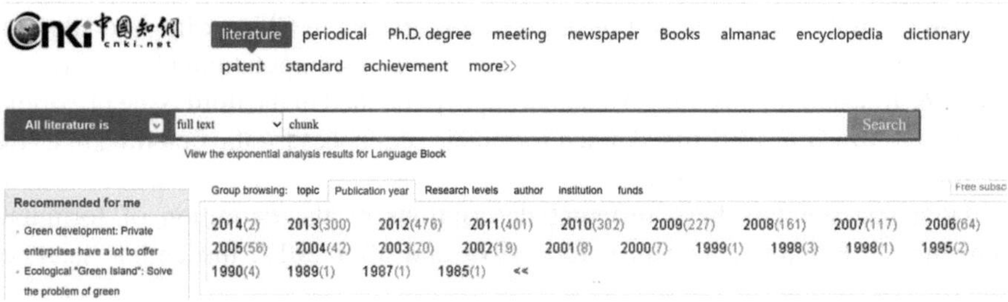

Fig. 1.1 Number of papers from CNKI searched by "formulaic sequences". *Note* CNKI = China National Knowledge Infrastructure

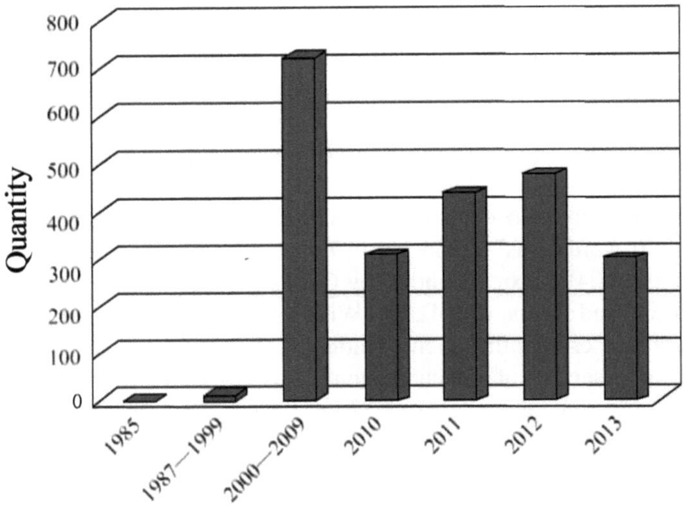

Fig. 1.2 Histogram of the number of papers searched by "formulaic sequences"

period. From 2010 to 2013, there were 302, 401, 476, and 300 papers each year. So far, the largest number was from 2012, amounting to 476 papers, and some papers in 2013 may not have been included in CNKI since this search was conducted on January 1, 2014. It can be seen that the domestic research on formulaic sequences has been in a straight upward trend.

The paper written by Lu Chuan and Liang Zhenhan, famous computational linguists and machine translation experts in China, in the third issue of *Journal of Chinese Information Processing* in 1987 is the earliest paper defining formulaic sequences in CNKI. The journal article "Analog Voice Privacy Systems Using TFSP Scrambling: Full Duplex and Half Duplex", which first mentioned the formulaic sequences in 1985, is a translation by Biwu (the pseudonym of the translator) of a paper by Cox and Tribolet (1983: 24), published in the first issue of *Bell System Technical Journal*. This study takes formulaic sequences as keywords and mentions them frequently. However, it does not give a clear definition to formulaic sequences. Both papers above are oriented to machine language, with a focus on formulaic sequences, fully indicating that the earliest researchers in China who paid attention to and translated "formulaic sequences" are experts in computational linguistics and machine translation. It is Yang Yuchen's paper published in the third issue of *Foreign Language World* in 1999 that defined formulaic sequences for the first time in CNKI by foreign language scholars.

Domestic scholars have different descriptions of the definition of formulaic sequences.[1] Excluding papers before 1999 and after 2012, the author searched

[1] In this book, the terms of "prefabricated formulaic sequences", "chunks" and others are all expressed as "formulaic sequences" for terminology uniformity and convenient for readers.

for the keywords "lexical chunk" and "lexical approach" (both meaning formulaic sequences) respectively in CNKI[2] and found that the definition of formulaic sequences in papers with citation frequency above 20 is divided into four categories, namely, authoritative definition, typical definition, cutting-edge definition and core definition with examples.

A. Authoritative definition

According to Pu (2003), a formulaic sequence is a frequently used, prefabricated, multi-word unit with a certain structure, expressing a certain meaning and allowing different degrees of abstraction. Wei (2004) points out that a formulaic sequence is a succession of meaningful word fragments of different lengths that appear in the corpus at high frequencies with a certain structure. According to Su and Lu (2010), a chunk refers to a syntactic-semantic aggregate of a construction that carries a semantic unit of that construction in a certain syntactic form in a relatively independent means.

B. Typical definition

Yang (1999) argues that formulaic sequences are those fixed and semi-fixed, patterned "plates" of structure, serving as the smallest units of human communication. Chang (2004) emphasizes that formulaic sequences are stored in the memory of language users as a whole and can be extracted directly when they are used, without grammatical generation and analysis. According to Duan (2008), formulaic sequences are multi-word units stored in the brain as a whole and can be used as prefabricated groups for extraction.

C. Cutting-edge definition

Wang and Zhang (2006) point out that formulaic sequences are meaningful sequential units of two or more words that can be automatically retrieved by the computer in the same form repeatedly. Luo and Xu (2007) stress that formulaic sequences are the product of balancing both semantic and syntactic structures. According to Lin (2011), machine-cut chunks are co-occurring sequences of more than two words extracted from the spoken corpus by computer software automatic cutting. Wang and Huang (2013) propose an operational definition that a sequence of words consisting of 2–6 words with a minimum frequency of 4, 4, 2, 2, 2, 2 (distributed in at least 2 texts), which has a certain degree of recognition in the native corpus and dictionaries and can express a relatively complete meaning.

D. Core definition

According to Qi (2005), formulaic sequences are special linguistic phenomena between grammar and vocabulary, which are usually stored in memory as a whole and are extracted directly when used without generating or analyzing according to grammatical rules. Chen (2008) states that formulaic sequences are linguistic phenomena that occur with high frequency in a form of more than single word in

[2] Other keywords were cited less than 20 times, and most of them were below 5.

real communication. Combining the advantages of grammar, semantics and context, they have a more fixed form. According to Li et al. (2012), formulaic sequences play an important role in communication in that their stable meaning collocation, fixed grammatical structure and specific discourse context integrate semantics, syntax and context, contributing to fluency and authentic word choice.

This book summarizes the main features of various definitions of formulaic sequences and their differences. The main features include (i) a combination of form and meaning/function; (ii) a high degree of reuse; (iii) individual whole units; and (iv) multi-word units.

(A) A combination of form and meaning/function

A formulaic sequence is a "combination of form and meaning/function". According to Jia (2004), formulaic sequences are characterized by formal wholeness and semantic agreement, combining the advantages of grammar, semantics and context. Therefore, they have more fixed grammatical structures, stable collocational meanings and specific pragmatic contexts. Long (2005) points out that formulaic sequences are lexico-grammatical units, which are paradigms acquired and preserved in long-term memory as a whole, including formulaic words and sentence patterns, and have more fixed grammatical structural restrictions as well as stable collocational meanings. Mao (2008) explains that formulaic sequence are combinations of multiple words with fixed or relatively fixed forms, with more complete structures, and relatively stable meanings and functions. According to Xu (2010), a formulaic sequence is a lexico-grammatical combination that is recognized, used, expresses meaning and achieves syntactic or communicative functions by language learners and users as a whole. It is a basic grammatical unit in constituting a sentence.

(B) High degree of reuse

The term "high degree of reuse" refers to the high frequency of repeated use of formulaic sequences. Zhou (2007) emphasizes that a formulaic sequence is a larger unit than a word that frequently appears in all kinds of sentences with a syntactic function. Jia and Du (2008) point out that a certain lexical sequence will be used as a conventional formulaic sequence if the constitutes co-occur frequently in a relatively stable form in terms of structure, and the sequence a more specific range in discourse function and meaning. According to Yuan and Guo (2010), the operational definition of a formulaic sequence is a string of two or more words as a whole; it is an idiomatic expression of convention in a fixed form, or a semi-fixed framework for sentence construction; it is a fixed phrase, or a collocation that occurs together with high frequency and does not need to be generated ad hoc according to grammatical rules; and there is no pause within the structure.

(C) Individual whole units

According to Yan (2003), formulaic sequences are language usage conventions characterized both grammatically and lexically, which are learned, used, and retained in memory as a whole. Huang and Wang (2011) state that formulaic sequences, which can be stored and extracted as a whole, have both lexical and grammatical features, and have specific expressive functions. According to Zhu (2012), the general definition of a formulaic sequence is a string of words that is memorized and extracted as a whole. This definition is actually given from the language user's perspective—whether the individual language user or learner sees it as a formulaic sequence and whether it is retained and extracted in memory as a whole. From the above literature, it can be seen that formulaic sequences are individual whole units.

(D) Multi-word units

Ding and Qi (2005) regard formulaic sequences as multi-word polywords that are closely related to the content but form units independently. According to Liu (2006), formulaic sequences are all multi-word units that are formally fixed and semantically prefabricated. Jiang (2008) points out that a formulaic sequence is a special polyword lexical phenomenon, including both relatively fixed combinations such as phrasal verbs, compounds, fixed collocations, idioms, phrases, etc. Phrase builders and sentence builders that can be opened on one or both sides are also included. Therefore, scholars consider a formulaic sequence as a "multi-word unit".

In addition to the main features above, there are still some divergences among scholars on the definition of formulaic sequences: (i) whether formulaic sequences are continuous or discontinuous; (ii) whether formulaic sequences include paragraphs and discourse.

(A) Whether formulaic sequences are continuous or discontinuous

According to Xu and Xu (2007), formulaic sequences are consecutive word fragments that are relatively well-structured, used at a certain frequency, and can express a certain meaning. Liu and Liu (2009) give this definition: consecutive word fragments of different lengths that occur more than five times in the COLEC. According to Wang and Qian (2009), the operational definition is a (non)continuous sequence of words consisting of 2–6 words with a minimum frequency of occurrence of 8, 6, 4, 2, and 2, respectively, that expresses a relatively complete meaning. Diao (2004) holds the view that a formulaic sequence is a linguistic phenomenon, in which two or more consecutive or non-consecutive words combined, with a higher frequency of co-occurrence of constituent words than random frequency, are capable of expressing a certain meaning in a relatively complete structure. Chen (2010) emphasizes that a formulaic sequence is a combination of two or more consecutive or non-consecutive words, which has a relatively stable semantic and syntactic structure and a certain sufficient frequency. When it is used, the whole formulaic sequence, with a mental reality, will be extracted from memory. Xue and Shi (2013) consider that a formulaic sequence is a substantive communication unit consisting of continuous or noncontinuous words or other meaningful elements pre-integrated into a module, with matching form and meaning/function. In the above examples, the first two definitions prescribe the words to be "continuous", while the last four "continuous or noncontinuous", showing that scholars have different views on this issue. In this book, formulaic sequences are taken as both continuous and discontinuous. This book only studies consecutive formulaic sequences, which are easier to be quickly retrieved and recognized by machine translation systems, and enable better translation matching.

(B) Whether formulaic sequences include paragraphs and discourse

According to Qian (2008), collocations, phrases, idioms, two-part allegorical sayings, proverbs, mottos, quotations, aphorisms, conversational sets, children's songs, lyrics, religious scriptures, etc. are linguistic structures composed of multiple words, stored, extracted and used as a whole, i.e., which are formulaic sequences referred to in this chapter. Ma (2011) defines formulaic sequences as multiple words that can be used independently to form sentences or discourse and achieve certain grammatical, discourse or pragmatic functions. They are also a minimal combination of form and meaning with grammatical, discourse or pragmatic functions. According to Zhan (2011), chunks are multi-word combinations in the lexicon that are used without syntactic analysis, including idioms, proverbs, clichés, verse, and high-frequency phrases in discourse. Wang (2012) indicates that in addition to multi-word collocations and sentence builders, formulaic sequences also include sentences and even discourses. As for Xue (2013), formulaic sequences are prefabricated language units that vary in linearity, length (from words to discourses), and frequency, combine syntactic, semantic, and contextual advantages, and have communicative, discursive, and pragmatic functions, which can be extracted directly without syntactic generation and analysis. From the above five papers, it can be seen that some scholars believe that formulaic sequences include paragraphs and discourses. However, as we can see from the definitions of formulaic sequences, most of the definitions refer to "formulaic sequences as multi-word units". Therefore, only multi-word units are considered as formulaic sequences, in which paragraphs and discourses are not included.

Studies on the definition of formulaic sequences for machine translation and business letters are insufficient and not easy to operate. Main achievements are as follows. Lu and Liang (1987) believe that the chunk consists of a head, the center, and adjuncts before and after it, which are considered as the specifier and the complement. There are only two kinds of chunks, case chunks and verb chunks respectively. Lin (1998) emphasizes that chunks are the elements that make up sentences. As Sun and Yu (2000) put it, formulaic sequences are non-recursive noun phrases, verb phrases, etc., and the concepts of chunk and phrases can be swapped. According to Jiang et al. (2007), a chunk is usually a complete linguistic unit, each word with a relatively bonding relationship, often occurring simultaneously. Zhou (2007) points out that a chunk is an information description unit through the combination of two or more words associated to a certain extent. According to Li and Huang (2013), a chunk is a grammatical structure, a non-recursive phrase that conforms to a certain grammatical function. Each chunk revolves around the center (head), with the center as the beginning or end. Li (2013) argues that a chunk is an important component of a sentence with non-transitive features that is intermediate between a lexicon and a sentence. These definitions need to be further refined and made more operational in order to be applied in the study on chunks for machine translation. There are also important studies on the definition of chunks for business letters. Zhang (2001) takes prefabricated chunks as lexico-grammatical units, in other words, lexical phrases in language. It is a multi-lexical phenomenon between traditional lexis and syntax. Li (2006) points out that lexical chunks are all structures larger than words that occur more frequently and have a more fixed form and meaning. According to Zhou (2010), chunks are the constituent units of natural language, and business English letters are written in the form of chunks rather than words. These three definitions of formulaic sequences for business letter are insufficient and difficult to operate.

In general, the academic community has actually gone through a long process of recognizing the importance of chunks, and now there is almost a consensus. Nevertheless, there are still many issues to be explored and recognized by the academic world. The definition of chunks is confusing and overly generalized, for example, hiatus, paragraph, and even whole chapter are considered as chunks. In addition, the definition of chunks for machine translation and business correspondence is not sufficient and not easy to operate. Therefore, there are still many problems that need to be solved in the study of chunks in China, and the ontological study of chunks should be strengthened, especially in the field of machine translation.

As Duan Shiping mentions in his article published in *Foreign Languages in China*, combination of formulaic sequences with construction grammar would be a trend of the foundation of formulaic sequence theory, while there is not enough research in China. Feng and Shi (2011) propose that on the basis of a large-scale corpus and empirical research, it is possible to dig into the relationship between formulaic sequences and construction grammar, combining the form and structure, function and typical contexts. Li and Pang (2008) argue that a formulaic sequence is deemed to be a special construction in construction grammar. Lu Jianming points out that the formulaic sequence needs to be recognized from the perspective of constructions, and it can be seen as an organic component of constructions. He argues that such an understanding is necessary in second language teaching and in Chinese information processing (Wang & Chen, 2009).

Goldberg (1995) proposes that a construction is composed of two or more symbolic units, in which form is in correspondence with meaning. Langacker (1987) sees words, morphemes, lexis and syntax as a continuum because continum contains more symbolic units and is more complex than formers, therefore requiring symbolic units and constructions to provide a unified explanation of grammar. Croft and Cruse (2004) emphasize that all human grammatical knowledge is essentially characterized by structure. These opinions seem to be valid, since constructions can be simple or complex, sticky or free, concrete words or structural patterns (Wang & Yin, 2007).

The concept of construction was introduced by Fillmore on the basis of frame semantics and expanded into a systematic theory by Goldberg. In 1995, Goldberg put forward the construction grammar, basic ideas including: (1) constructions are a combination of form and meaning; (2) constructions can express grammatical meaning and have unique semantic structural relations; (3) neither the form nor the meaning of a construction can be directly inferred from its constituents or other constructions (Goldberg, 1995, 2006, 2009). The starting point of construction grammar is to study the combination of form and meaning, and later Goldberg added function, which became the combination of form and meaning/function. Yan (2006) points out that constructions are more than "free form" idioms, and abstract sentence patterns, and even morphemes (with affixes) and words are included. Various conventionalized combinations of "form and meaning/function" are all constructions, at all levels of language. Morphemes, words, compounds, and fully fixed idioms are called fixed constructions, which are lexically fixed (i.e., their components are irreplaceable), while constructions below semi-fixed idioms are schematic constructions. These two kinds of constructions differ in that fixed constructions have only one instance, while the schematic constructions more than one instance due to the partially or fully open lexical parts.

Goldberg and Suttle (2010) clarify that the main distinction between various schools of construction grammar is the emphasis and the use of symbols, including the Sign-based Construction Grammar (SBCG), Fluid Construction Grammar (FCxG), Cognitive Grammar (CG), Embodied Construction Grammar (ECxG), Radical Construction Grammar (RCxG), Cognitive Construction Grammar (CCxG), and Simpler Syntax (SS). The concept of "constructions", which emphasize the correspondence between meaning and form, has long been proposed in cognitive linguistics. With deeper understanding of the nature of constructions and the deepening analysis of schematic constructions, "patterns are stored as constructions even if they are fully predictable as long as they occur with sufficient frequency" (Goldberg, 2006). Liu (2010) further distinguishes between grammatical and rhetorical constructions. The former refers to any kind of constructions whose constructional meaning can be deduced from the constituents, as well as those fully grammaticalized constructions, the constructional meaning of which cannot be deduced, while rhetorical constructions involve all non-deducible constructions, only if such non-deducibility has not been fully grammaticalized in the constructions. Grammatical and rhetorical constructions form a continuum, which is a new development in understanding constructions (Xue & Shi, 2013). Construction grammar originates from but is independent of cognitive grammar. Although cognitive linguistics also considers the construction as a unit of grammar with an emphasis on its integrity, it had not attracted sufficient awareness and attention to the integrity of constructions. However, the introduction of "unpredictability" has brought the integrity of constructions into focus. Since this unpredictability fully reflects the Gestalt theory that "the whole is greater than the combination of parts", providing evidence for the argument that the overall meaning of the construction is greater than the meaning of the combination of parts. Therefore, domestic research on construction grammar has adopted the idea of Goldberg (Zhang, 2013).

The classical definition of a construction given by Goldberg (1995) is that "C is a CONSTRUCTION iff def C is a form-meaning pair such that some aspects of Fi or some aspects of Si is not strictly predictable from C's components parts or from other previously established constructions." According to this definition, constructions cover almost all linguistic units from morphemes, words, idioms, and phrases to sentences, each regarded as a complete structure independently. Construction grammar further extends "form-meaning pairs" to "form and meaning/function pairs" (Goldberg, 2003, 2006). Since morphemes and some monomorphemic words do not have structure in a general sense, Goldberg later restricted constructions to structured linguistic units (Goldberg, 2009).

A chunk is a combination of form and meaning/function. In this regard, it is identical to constructions. Xue and Shi (2013) summarize the basic understanding of constructions in the academic world, and give a new position to the connotation of the chunk, and elucidate the basic properties through comparison with the constructions. In terms of the nature, the chunk equates to a construction; in terms of the expression system, the chunk is highly prefabricated; in terms of the immediate processing of communication, it is an individual whole unit in essence; in terms of the grammatical status, it is a mediator between lexis and syntax; in terms of the morphosyntactic relationship, it is not completely transparent and there is a cross-relationship between chunks and the constructions; in terms of the relationship between the members, it belongs to prototypic category, and different types and specific chunks often show the feature of family resemblance.

Chunks are prefabricated in the memory system and are extracted as a whole by the communicator in a specific language situations and then combined and processed as required by expression. In this way, the semantic integrity of such units in the communicative process is ensured and the speed of language output is increased, thus achieving the unity of accuracy and fluency. And the constructive feature is the fundamental embodiment of the specific communicative function of chunks. In this regard, chunks are the principal part of constructions. The phenomenon of "construction cult" seems to prevail in the current research on construction grammar, which believes that all language problems are related to constructions, and that the construction theory, worshipped as a panacea, can explain everything (Shi, 2014). However, any theory or methodology works by discovering and constructing some questions, and then trying to analyze and solve them. Through a particular theory, a linguistic phenomenon is possibly turned into a linguistic fact in the light of a certain theory, and even into a linguistic fact, in other words, linguistic components and relations defined, discovered or predicted under a particular hypothesis or theory (Shi, 2013).

As mentioned above, definitions of chunks is chaotic, and the boundary of constructions is unclear.[3] Chunks and constructions are regarded as panacea by some scholars. This book believes that no single theory can be all-inclusive. Both chunks and constructions have their own advantages and limitations, which should be the basis of the study of the chunk definition model of business English letters in MT.

1.3 Research on MT-Oriented Chunks

Compared with human translation, MT relies on computers to simulate human's recognizing, understanding and translation of languages, in which machines could replace or assist human translation in order to eliminate language barriers and realize smooth communication.

[3] Discrepancies on the boundary of the members of the constructions category still exist at present. This book agrees with Lu Jianming that the constructions are at sentence-level.

MT is a highly challenging topic with significant application value. The urgent need for efficient and fast translation in the information age motivates MT development. In 1949, W. Weaver, vice president of the Rockefeller Foundation, proposed code-interpreting methods for MT in his memo entitled "Translation", addressing some methodological issues, including multiple meanings of linguistic units, and argued that languages have universals extensively at the linguistic level. In 1954, Georgetown University, with the assistance of IBM (International Business Machines Corporation), gave the first public demonstration of English-Russian machine translation. They used an IBM-701 computer to translate 50 Russian sentences into English with an English-Russian MT system, demonstrating the feasibility of MT to the public and the scientific community. Throughout the 1950s and 1960s, research on MT was showing a positive upward trend. Many researchers believed that fully automated MT would soon be possible as long as there was ample linguistic data. However, since they underestimated the complexity and enormity of natural language as well as translation itself, the quality of machine translation did not get any better as MT scaled up. There were a lot of jokes, such as translating "The mountain is 2,000 feet high." into "山有2000只脚。" (meaning that the mountain has 2000 physical feet.) Therefore, some people assert that MT is always a machine that makes "translation jokes".

The development of MT was marked by the first machine translation experiments using IBM computers at Georgetown University in 1954. However, the report conducted by the ALPAC (Automatic Language Processing Advisory Committee of the National Academy of Sciences) in 1964 brought MT research into a slump. In 1966, ALPAC issued a report in 1966 entitled "Languages and machines: computers in translation and linguistics", also known as the ALPAC report. It took a negative view of MT and recommended a drastic reduction in its funding. Although the report had a significant negative impact on MT at that time, its criteria of "intelligibility" and "fidelity" for evaluating machine translations are still widely used today. After the report, MT in many countries was stagnant due to policy and funding difficulties, except for a few groups in France, Japan, Canada and others. In the mid-1970s, MT began revitalizing. With the emergence of the linguistic theory established by Noam Chomsky, rule-based MT came on stage and got mature, and many MT systems appeared in the market. In 1976, the European Economic Community (EEC) purchased SYSTRAN, a machine translation system developed by Georgetown University, as their translation tool to conduct multilingual machine translation for English, French, German, Spanish, Italian, Portuguese, etc. TAUM-METEO, an English-French MT system developed jointly by Université de Montréa and the Government of Canada Translation Bureau, was put into operation for weather forecasting in 1977, which required no human assistance and produced relatively high-quality translations. The EC started the MT program EUROTRA in 1982 in an attempt to achieve mutual translation in all of its official languages. In the early 1980s, the ODA (Official Development Assistance) program, organized by the Japanese Ministry of International Trade and Industry in cooperation with its four neighboring Asian countries, conducted research on multilingual MT for five languages: Japanese, Chinese, Indonesian, Malaysian, and Thai. However, the end of EUROTRA and ODA programs was announced in the early 1990s, and neither achieved expected results.

MT research in China initiated in 1956. Later, Beijing Foreign Language Institute (now Beijing Foreign Studies University), South China Institute of Technology (now South China University of Technology), Harbin Institute of Technology, etc. established MT research groups respectively and carried out experiments. In the mid-1970s, MT research in China advanced to recovery, and the Institute of Linguistics of the Chinese Academy of Social Sciences began to train graduate students specializing in MT. Around the late 1980s, a series of commercialized MT systems were introduced to the market, such as "TRANS—STAR I" in Beijing, "Internet V2.0" in Tianjin, "Langwei" in Shaanxi, etc.

From the late 1980s to the 1990s, corpus-based MT emerged and has made substantial development since 1999. This approach is based on a large-scale collection of bilingual corpora, which are parallel texts. Therefore, it uses a corpus as the source of the translation knowledge.

The corpus-based approaches are divided into example-based machine translation (EBMT) and statistics-based machine translation (SBMT). The first approach gets translations by imitating the most similar translation examples in a bilingual corpus while the second advocates building a mathematical model of the translation process, estimating the model parameters based on bilingual corpus, and doing the translation with the model and the estimated parameters. In "A Framework for Japanese-English Machine Translation Using the Principle of Analogy" in 1984, Makoto Nagao, Japanese machine translation expert, analyzes the basic process of translating sentences for foreign language beginners. He points out that in the process of translating, human beings first decompose the input sentence into fragments (e.g., chunks), which would be translated into another language, and finally combined into a long sentence in accordance with the analogy principle. Example-based MT and translation memory (TM) are relatively similar and sometimes indistinguishable, both identifying, extracting and comparing the similarities and differences between the example and translations in order to select the best translation. However, the selection in TM depends on the translator. In example-based MT, the program identifies the corresponding phrase fragments and reassemble them to form the sentence in the target language (Feng & Hu, 2012).

In example-based MT, the main source of knowledge is the parallel example database (such as the bilingual chunk bank[4]), which mainly has two fields: one keeping the chunk of the source language and the other keeping the corresponding translation. Whenever a sentence in the source language is input, the system compares the chunks with those in the source language in the database, finds the most similar ones, and outputs the sentence in the target language by imitating the translation of the corresponding chunks. In the bilingual chunk bank, translation knowledge is represented as examples, which are easy to add or delete and simple to maintain. High-quality translations will be produced when a larger bilingual chunk bank is utilized and precisely compared, in order to eliminate the drawbacks of rule-based

[4] The ideal bilingual counterpart granularity is considered to be chunks in this book.

MT that must perform deep linguistic analysis. Studies on corresponding chunks are of crucial importance for MT because corresponding bilingual chunks are extremely valuable sources of translation knowledge. However, the smaller the utilized chunks are, the more ambiguity cases there will be, leading to a decrease in translation quality. For this reason, a set of corresponding rules should be established to determine whether two chunks can correspond (Feng & Hu, 2012). Consequently, the study on corresponding bilingual chunks needs to focus on the correspondence between chunks and the corresponding rules, which are pivotal to the research on example-based MT.

Currently, the chunk analysis techniques for MT have become an important branch in natural language and have received widespread attention, driven by both related language processing research and information processing technology applications. As a representative of shallow parsing, chunk analysis is dedicated to identifying components with relatively simple structures and important functions and meanings in a sentence. It is limited to parsing sentences into smaller units without revealing their syntactic relationships (Li & Huang, 2013). Abney (1996) proposed to divide syntactic parsing into multiple stratums, each outputting only one result, while within each stratum only simple finite-state automata are used for analysis. This is a study of full syntactic parsing based on chunk analysis. Watanabe et al. (2003) implemented a chunk-based statistical MT model for Japanese-English, also suggesting a possible direction for the application of English-Chinese chunks, in which the full syntactic parsing is not the purpose and it is chunks instead of words or phrases that achieve specific applications. Backed by lexical knowledge base, Zhou (2008) automatically obtains all the word-based basic block rules from an annotated corpus, and automatically excludes a large number of low-reliable and invalid rules by setting the confidence level. For the low-reliability rules with high-frequency, internal lexical constraints and external contextual restriction knowledge are continuously introduced to gradually make it evolve into structured rules with stronger descriptive power. Tsinghua University has done a lot of work in organizing and processing chunks, while building a system of chunk division: basic chunks, functional chunks, and recognition of event description small sentence. Zhou et al. (2001) point out that all current chunk information is annotated by human beings. Using macro commands in Word to define different shortcut keys, one-click input for each chunk can be realized, which greatly improves the annotation efficiency. According to preliminary statistics, the annotation speed before was about 120 words per hour. With the familiarity of the annotation specification and the processing, the speed has been increasing to basically reach 240 words per hour after 1–2 months. Zhou Qiang was the first scholar to propose the term "chunk bank" and has done a series of researches, but all of them are on Chinese chunks. In 2002, Yao Tianshun of Northeastern University extended the monolingual chunk to meet the practical needs of MT, and defined a kind of unambiguous and nestable translation unit with semantic self-sufficiency and conversion adequacy as the bilingual extended chunk (Liu & Yang, 2004).

According to Jiang et al. (2007), the chunk-based translation approach helps to solve the ambiguity in MT. All sentences are required to be analyzed into different types of chunks. However, the current technology cannot manage the countless chunks, and it is even difficult to determine the boundaries of each type. Some of these chunks consist of two words or even more than 10 words. However, Jiang does not specify the type of chunks, and the granule was too large (more than 10 words) with a low repetition to allow the computer to accurately identify rule-based and appropriate chunks, thus failing to ensure the extraction of valid chunks. Jiang et al. (2007) also state that these chunks cause unsuitable structures mainly due to the existing filtering rules with insufficient constraint descriptions, i.e., the linguistic knowledge described is inadequate. Although the existing filtering rules help to resolve some common errors on the boundaries of chunks, they cannot determine the validity of the internal structure of chunks.

According to Cheng et al. (2003), chunk-based processing is a new approach in natural language processing in recent years. However, in order to apply it to spoken-language translation, it is necessary to make a reasonable definition of bilingual chunks according to the characteristics of spoken language. Taking the existing definitions of monolingual chunks as the foundation, they propose a bilingual chunk concept at both syntactic and semantic levels in terms of the differences between Chinese and English as well as the features of interpretation, and give a detailed analysis of its characteristics. Meanwhile, they also designed a bilingual chunk processing method combining automatic computer division and manual proofreading for the Chinese-English parallel corpora. They applied the method to bilingual chunk division and alignment of Chinese-English sentence-level aligned spoken corpus, and thus conducted experiments on bilingual chunk-based statistical MT of spoken language. It turns out that their definition of bilingual chunks meets the practical needs of interpretation, and the bilingual chunk-based corpus processing method can effectively improve the performance of the spoken-language translation system. Cheng et al. (2004) puts forward an automatic bilingual chunk identification algorithm, which combine statistics and rules to automatically analyze the bilingual chunks in parallel corpora. With this method, supplemented by manual proofreading, it is convenient to attain the parallel corpora and bilingual chunk banks containing bilingual chunks. Chunk recognition is the basis for the implementation of the "chunk-based processing". The results of their experiments on a 60,000-sentence spoken corpus in hotel reservation are conducive to the optimization of the bilingual chunk alignment algorithm. These two papers propose the concept of bilingual chunks, investigates bilingual chunk processing method that combines automatic computer division and manual proofreading with the spoken language in hotel reservation as the subject in a Chinese-English bilingual chunk bank. However, both papers are based on spoken language, and the applicability to written language needs to be further explored.

In discussing tools and methods for chunk extraction in corpus, Zhan (2011) points out that tools and techniques for language retrieval in natural language processing have progressed rapidly, and that techniques for chunk recognition have developed from artificial recognition to machine recognition. Zhou et al. (2005) designs an algorithm based on multi-layer filtering, requiring no sentence annotation, no syntactic analysis, no lexical analysis, or even no word separation of Chinese sentences. According to test results, the accuracy of chunk extraction is $F = 0.70$ and the accuracy of alignment is F = 0.80, manifesting that this algorithm has a good performance. Moreover, compared with the word-based system, the aligned bilingual chunks obtained by this algorithm are used in a statistical MT system, and the results show that the translation ability of the chunk-based MT has been significantly improved. Zhang et al. (2006) obtain translation head-phrase according to dictionary-based word alignment which is very reliable, and determines statistical translation boundary based on the translation extending reliability. All candidate translations of source language phrase are extracted by combining translation head-phrase with statistical translation boundary. A linear combination model is applied to evaluate all candidate translations of source language phrase and the most probable one is selected. Results show that the performance of their proposed phrase alignment method is better than other methods. Among these three papers, the first one summarizes and reviews the chunk identification and retrieval techniques and tools for English from the perspective of corpus, without corpus data-driven research and practical validation; the second one, oriented to statistical MT, investigates the automatic extraction and alignment of bilingual chunks in Chinese and English sentences; and the third one uses the results of dictionary alignment with high reliability to determine the translation head-phrase for Chinese phrases. In conclusion, most of the studies on bilingual corresponding chunks focus on techniques, and the correspondence relations and rules for business-letter-oriented MT based on translation facts have rarely been explored.

It is an increasing trend of developing professional translation systems based on constrained languages for users in specific fields. For example, CSK in Tokyo, Japan, launched the ARGO program which translates Japanese stock market reports into English, and the Institute of Computational Linguistics of Peking University in China, the Institute of Computing Technology of the Chinese Academy of Sciences, and the National Key Laboratory of Computer Science and Artificial Intelligence of Tsinghua University jointly developed a Chinese-English MT system for journalism.

Li (2010), in his discussion on the design of parallel corpora and the identification of corresponding units, points out that the purpose of the study is to determine the corresponding unit identification procedure and build a corresponding unit database by developing parallel corpora. Based on the newly constructed parallel corpora conducted by Shanghai Jiao Tong University, Li and Zhao (2013) conducted a study on the identification and application of corresponding sequences, which are an important resource for translation strategy exploration, translation unit database construction, and bilingual dictionary compilation. If the data resources are sufficient, MT in real texts from multiple domains could also be realized. Nevertheless, the practical application of correspondence sequences still needs to be further researched and developed, and theoretical and technical problems to be solved.

On the basis of previous studies, the research on English-Chinese business letter chunks in MT in this book provides theoretical, technical and methodological support for the construction of the corresponding chunk bank, and aims to improve the translation accuracy of English-Chinese business letter. Next, we will discuss the research on business-letter-oriented chunks.

1.4 Research on Business-Letter-Oriented Chunks

Since most of the international business communications are carried out in the form of letters, the bilingual corpus of English-Chinese business letters contributes to the acquisition of translation knowledge, and its quality largely affects business communication and exchange. When translating such texts, bilingual corresponding sequences for translation is beneficial to represent the unique style and language characteristics of business letters, which makes target texts more authentic. Therefore, chunks should be paid great attention for better business letter translation. However, only a few scholars have conducted studies on this area at present.

Zhou and Liao (2008) divide the business English letter chunks into four categories according to their cohesive function in discourse: (1) Multi-word combinations such as "wing to" and "firm offer", which were traditionally classified as phrases and now are considered as a form of textual cohesion, as a whole not only in terms of comprehension but also of writing; (2) Phrasal constraints, shorter phrases that can be filled in the blanks, such as "for your reference", "an offer subject to", etc.; (3) Institutionalized utterances, which can be stored as a whole by the speaker, including aphorisms, polite formula in foreign trade and others, such as "as requested, …" "enclosed please find…" etc.; and (4) Sentence builders, referring to the lexical phrases that provide the framework for the whole sentence, such as "We are looking forward to…" and "We thank you for…". The above categorization uses Nattinger and DeCarrico's chunk classification[5] for reference. But they only provide corresponding examples in the letters, without developing a new classification based on the characteristics of business letters.

Also based on Nattinger and DeCarrico's classification, Zhang (2013) classifies 370 business English letters in *THE AMA HANDBOOK OF BUSINESS ENGLISH LETTERS* published by the AMA Association into four categories: competitive letters, collaborative letters, conflictive letters and convivial letters. Ten letters from each category are listed as samples for analysis. After analyzing the labeled lexical chunks in terms of the number of chunks, the number of words and frequency, it is found that: (1) the frequency of chunks in business English letters is pretty high, with one chunk appearing every 5–6 words; (2) in terms of form, polywords contain a large number of terminology and business jargon; (3) from the perspective of function, the use of lexical chunks in business English letters contributes to the accuracy and politeness of language and helps learners to write authentic business English letters. However, this research only provides insights into the teaching and learning of business English, and only 40 examples of business English letters are used, so the corpus is small and the data is not convincing enough.

Pang (2011) selects 40 English business letters for analysis, of which twenty pieces are from foreign trade companies in daily use and twenty from students' writing in school. It is found that the frequency of chunks in business English letters is quite high in practical use, with one chunk in seven words on average. According to Nattinger

[5] Polywords, conventionalized or institutionalized expression, phrasal constraints and sentence builders.

and DeCarrico's classification, phrasal constraints, polywords, and conventionalized expressions are the most frequent chunks used in sentence builders. The frequency of chunks in students' business English letters is relatively low, with an average of one chunk in 11 words. Even though the corpus selected in this research are authentic materials, the scale is too small to produce statistically valid data.[6]

Although there is little research on the application of chunks in business letter translation, its role in translation has been investigated by scholars. According to Yuan (2009), chunks are treated as a translation unit, and sufficient chunks and knowledge of chunking can not only help translators achieve successful unmarked translation with fluency and accuracy, but also enable translators to do more marked translations.

According to Zhou (2010), a business English letter is usually written in a formal form used for external contact between business organizations and between business organizations and their clients, involving business relations, negotiations, and communications. Therefore, writing steps and conventional phrases in business English letters have been fixed, such as "we owe your name and address to…" and "subject to…". Since these phrases and jargons appear frequently with fixed form and meaning and the context is settled, a scientific analysis is necessary and feasible, of which the results also play an important role in understanding the linguistic features of business English letters.

Zhou (2010) divides business English chunks into three categories: (1) Words or polywords like "herewith" and "by the way", which, traditionally, were seen as phrases, but now they are regarded as special forms of polywords as a form of discourse cohesion as a whole; (2) Phrasal constraints, usually less long chunks that can be filled in the blanks, such as "as to…" and "an offer subject to…"; (3) Institutionalized utterances, referring to linguistic blocks stored as a whole, including aphorisms, polite formula in foreign trade and fixed sentence patterns, such as "as requested". Zhou He also points out that the language of business English letters has obvious features of chunks, which is the result of its long-term use in business activities.

However, the examples in the above are not appropriate, because some instances are not chunks in my opinion, such as "herewith" and "as to…". The reason lies in the lack of a clear definition of business letter chunks.

From the perspective of MT, the usage of terms in business English letters translation will be obtained as long as these corresponding chunks are matched appropriately. In this sense, whether the machine translations of English-Chinese business letters is authentic and whether the accuracy is improved or not depends on the correct use of these English-Chinese business corresponding chunks.

In conclusion, although a few scholars probed into business letter chunks, they mainly focused on second language acquisition with less research corpus. At present,

[6] According to Liu (1999), the data collected cannot be less than 30, otherwise technical processing must be performed to be statistically significant.

almost no scholars have yet combined quantitative and qualitative methods to MT-oriented research on English-Chinese business letter corresponding chunks based on a larger unlabeled corpus using construction grammar.

1.5 Summary

In this chapter, we have made a comprehensive analysis on the definition of chunks, and classifies the definitions given by domestic scholars into authoritative definitions, typical definitions, cutting-edge definition and core definitions. Then we summarize the main features of chunks: (i) a combination of form and meaning/function; (ii) a high degree of reuse; (iii) individual whole units; and (iv) multi-word units. At present, there are still discrepancies in the definition of chunks, mainly: (i) whether chunks are continuous or discontinuous; (ii) whether chunks include paragraphs and discourse. In this book, it is considered that chunks are "continuous" because they are a combination of form and meaning/function, and from the perspective of MT, continuous chunks are easier to operate for bilingual counterparts and have better match of translation. Finally, chunks are "multi-word units" and should not include paragraphs and discourses.

Chunks are complex, which makes the research challenging but exciting at the same time (Wang & Chen, 2012). Influenced by the idea that chunks can explain everything (Li, 2011), the definition of chunks is confusing and over-generalized in China. The definition of chunks for machine translation and business letters is insufficient and uneasy to operate. In general, there are still problems in domestic studies on chunks. It is suggested that the ontological study on chunks be strengthened, especially in MT. Besides, most of the studies on bilingual corresponding chunks focus on techniques, and the correspondence relations and rules for business-letter-oriented MT based on translation facts have rarely been explored. Although a few scholars probed into business letter chunks, they mainly focused on second language acquisition with less research corpus. At present, almost no scholars have yet combined quantitative and qualitative methods to MT-oriented research on English-Chinese business letter corresponding chunks based on a larger unlabeled corpus using construction grammar.

The reason why English-Chinese business letters are selected in this book including: first, there are a wealth of phrases and corresponding Chinese translations, such as "supply from stock", "regular customers", and "within the contracted time". From the perspective of MT, the accuracy of MT will be improved and translations of English-Chinese business letters will be more authentic as long as these corresponding chunks are matched appropriately; second, with China's growth of economy, the business interactions between China and foreign countries are increasing, resulting in more application of business letters. As English is the common working language, the English-Chinese business correspondence is an important means to carry out foreign economic and trade business as well as related activities. The translation of business English letters involves all aspects of foreign trade, and it is also a basic skill that practitioners must master. Therefore, the study on English-Chinese business letter chunks is not only beneficial but also practical, with research significance and practical value.

The study on MT-oriented corresponding chunks in English-Chinese business letters can provide theoretical, technical and methodological support for the construction of the corresponding chunk banks, which can further improve the translation accuracy of the system. The achievements can be used in the machine translation of English-Chinese business letters to solve the language barriers in communication, thus promoting the domestic foreign trade and economic exchanges. Therefore, this book attempts to explore this aspect.

References

Abney, S. (1996). Part of speech tagging and partial parsing. In K. Church, S. Young, & G. Bloothooft (Eds.), *Corpus-based methods in language and speech* (pp. 119–136). Kluwer Academic Publishers.

Altenberg, B. (1998). On the phraseology of spoken English: The evidence of recurrent word combinations. In A. Cowie (Ed.), *Phraseology: Theory, analysis and applications* (pp. 101–122). Oxford University Press.

Becker, J. (1975). *The phrasal lexical.* Bolt and Newman.

Biber, D., et al. (1999). *Longman grammar of spoken and written English.* Longman.

Bolinger, D. (1975). Meaning and memory. *Forum Linguisticum, 1*, 2–14.

Brown, R. (1973). *A first language: The early stages.* Harvard University Press.

Chang, C. (2004). The function of formulaic language. *Foreign Languages and Their Teaching, 2*, 7–10.

Chen, W. (2008). Enhancing students' lexical chunk awareness to improve writing skills. *Foreign Language World, 3*, 48–53.

Chen, Y. (2010). Lexical chunk studies and compilation of English learning dictionaries. *Foreign Language Learning Theory and Practice, 4*, 28–34.

Cheng, W., Zhao, J., Liu, F., et al. (2004). Automatic recognition of bilingual chunks for oral translation. *Chinese Journal of Computers, 8*, 1016–1020.

Cheng, W., Zhao, J., Xu, B., et al. (2003). A method for bilingual chunk processing in Chinese-English oral translation. *Journal of Chinese Information Processing, 2*, 21–27.

Cortes, V. (2004). Lexical bundles in published and student disciplinary writing: Examples from history and biology. *English for Specific Purposes, 3*, 397–423.

Cowie, A. P. (1998). Multi-word lexical units and communicative language teaching. In P. Arnaud & H. Bejoint (Eds.), *Vocabulary and applied linguistics* (pp. 152–161). Macmillan.

Cox, R. V. & Tribolet, J. M. (1983). Analog voice privacy systems using TFSP scrambling: Full duplex and half duplex. *BSTJ, 62*(1), 24–32.

Croft, W., & Cruse, D. A. (2004). *Cognitive linguistics.* Cambridge University Press.

Diao, L. (2004). Lexical chunk competence investigation of English majors. *Journal of PLA University of Foreign Languages, 2004*(4), 35–38.

Ding, Y., & Qi, Y. (2005). Correlation study on lexical chunk application and English speaking and writing level. *Journal of PLA University of Foreign Languages, 3*, 49–53.

Duan, S. (2008). Review of research on second language chunk teaching in China. *Foreign Languages in China, 4*, 63–74.

Ellis, R. (1985). *Understanding second language acquisition.* Oxford University Press.

Ellis, N. C. (1996). Sequencing in SLA: Phonological memory, chunking and points of order. *Studies in Second Language Acquisition, 18*, 91–126.

Feng, Z., & Hu, F. (2012). *Mathematical linguistics* (revised ed.). The Commercial Press.
Feng, S., & Shi, C. (2011). On "trinity grammar" in Chinese teaching. *Linguistic Sciences, 5,* 464–472.
Fillmore, C., et al. (1979). On fluency. In C. Fillmore (Ed.), *Individual differences in language ability and language behavior* (pp. 93–102). Academic Press.
Goldberg, E. (1995). *Constructions: A construction grammar approach to argument structure.* The University of Chicago Press.
Goldberg, E. (2003). Constructions: A new theoretical approach to language. *Journal of Foreign Languages, 3,* 1–11.
Goldberg, E. (2006). *Constructions at work.* Oxford University Press.
Goldberg, E. (2009). Constructions at work. *Cognitive Linguistics, 20*(1), 201–224.
Goldberg, A., & Suttle, L. (2010). Construction grammar. *Wiley Interdisciplinary Reviews: Cognitive Science, 4,* 468–477.
Huang, Y., & Wang, H. (2011). "Chinese scene" in second language chunk: Current status and prospects. *Foreign Language World, 3,* 74–81.
Hunston, S., & Francis, G. (1999). *Pattern grammar—A corpus-driven approach to the lexical grammar of English.* John Benjamins Publishing Company.
Jia, L. (2004). Lexical chunk theory and its implications for second language proficiency development. *Journal of Jianghan University (Social Sciences Edition), 1,* 102–105.
Jia, G., & Du, Y. (2008). Study on structure and function of Chinese "chunks." *Journal of College of Chinese Language and Culture of Jinan University, 2,* 64–70.
Jiang, Y. (2008). An empirical study on lexical chunk teaching to enhance English learners' oral communication. *Journal of University of International Relations, 3,* 86–90.
Jiang, B., Zhang, Q., Shen, Y., et al. (2007). Research on automatic extraction of Chinese chunks for machine-aided translation. *Journal of Chinese Information Processing, 1,* 9–16.
Keller, R. (1979). Gambits: Conversational strategy signals. *Journals of Pragmatics, 3,* 219–238.
Krashen, S., & Scarcella, R. (1978). On routines and patterns in language acquisition and performance. *Language Learning, 28*(2), 283–300.
Lancker-Sidtis, D., & Rallon, G. (2004). Tracking the incidence of formulaic expressions in everyday speech: Methods for classification and verification. *Language and Communication, 2,* 207–240.
Langacker, R. W. (1987). *Foundations of cognitive grammar: Theoretical prerequisites* (Vol. 1). Stanford University Press.
Lewis, M. (1993). *The lexical approach: The state of ELT and a way forward.* Language Teaching Publications.
Lewis, M. (1997). *Implementing the lexical approach: Putting theory into practice.* Language Teaching Publications.
Li, T. (2006). Advantages and productive training of lexical chunks in foreign trade English writing teaching. *Foreign Language World, 1,* 34–39.
Li, W. (2010). Design of parallel corpus and identification of corresponding units. *Contemporary Foreign Languages Studies, 9,* 22–27.
Li, J. (2011). Review of domestic and foreign chunk studies. *Shandong Foreign Language Teaching, 5,* 17–23.
Li, S. (2013). Research and development in natural language processing. *Journal of Yanshan University (Philosophy and Social Science Edition), 5,* 376–384.
Li, Y., & Huang, H. (2013). Overview of Chinese chunk analysis studies. *Journal of Chinese Information Processing, 3,* 1–8.
Li, J., Li, L., & Gao, X. (2012). Lexical chunk research from the perspective of hermeneutics. *Foreign Language Research, 6,* 74–78.
Li, T., & Pang, J. (2008). Cognitive mechanism of formulaic language from the perspective of construction grammar. *Journal of Xidian University (Social Science Edition), 1,* 141–146.
Li, J., & Zhao, X. (2013). Research on recognition and application of corresponding word sequences in parallel texts. *Technology Enhanced Foreign Languages, 5,* 36–40.
Lin, X. (1998). Semantic study of Chinese information field. *Applied Linguistics, 3,* 94–97.

Lin, W. (2011). Theoretical and empirical study on the characteristics of position markers of machine-cut chunks. *Foreign Languages in China, 5*, 33–39.
Liu, R. (1999). *Research methods in foreign language teaching*. Foreign Language Teaching and Research Press.
Liu, J. (2006). Lexical chunks and college oral English teaching. *Shandong Foreign Language Teaching, 4*, 88–90.
Liu, D. (2010). From syntactic constructions to rhetorical constructions (Part 1). *Contemporary Rhetoric, 3*, 7–17.
Liu, X., & Liu, X. (2009). Chunk structure types and pragmatic functions in written Chinese of college students based on corpus. *Foreign Languages in China, 2*, 48–53.
Liu, D., & Yang, E. (2004). A new bilingual chunk correspondence algorithm. *Computer Development & Applications, 3*, 2–6.
Long, S. (2005). Extraction advantages of prefabricated chunks. *Journal of Lanzhou Institute of Education, 4*, 49–57.
Lu, C., & Liang, Z. (1987). Rule-based Chinese for information processing. *Journal of Chinese Information Processing, 3*, 17–24.
Luo, X., & Xu, L. (2007). Semantic "matching" and translation teaching. *Foreign Language Teaching and Research, 5*, 386–391.
Ma, G. (2011). Definition, classification, and recognition of lexical chunks. *Journal of PLA University of Foreign Languages, 1*, 1–4.
Mao, C. (2008). Features of chunk use in English learners' conversations. *Journal of PLA University of Foreign Languages Institute, 2*, 58–62.
Moon, R. (1997). Vocabulary connections: Multi-word items in English. In N. Schmitt & M. McCarthy (Eds.), *Vocabulary: Description, acquisition, & pedagogy* (pp. 40–63). Cambridge University Press.
Nattinger, J. R. (1988). Some current trends in vocabulary teaching. In M. J. McCarthy & R. A. Carter (Eds.), *Vocabulary and language teaching* (pp. 62–85). Longman.
Nattinger, J., & DeCarrico, J. (1992). *Lexical phrases and language teaching*. Oxford University Press.
Pang, X. (2011). *Chunks and business English letters*. Master's thesis, Ocean University of China.
Pawley, A., & Syder, F. H. (1983). Two puzzles for linguistic theory: Native-like selection and native-like fluency. In J. Richards & R. Schmidt (Eds.), *Language and communication* (pp. 191–225). Longman.
Peters, A. (1983). *The units of language acquisition*. Cambridge University Press.
Pu, J. (2003). Collocation, connection, and lexical chunks in English vocabulary teaching. *Foreign Language Teaching and Research, 6*, 438–445.
Qi, Y. (2005). Prefabricated Chunks and College English Writing. *Shandong Foreign Language Teaching, 5*, 64–66.
Qian, X. (2008). Preliminary study on Chinese lexical chunks. *Journal of Peking University (Philosophy & Social Sciences), 5*, 139–146.
Renouf, A., & Sinclair, J. (1991). Collocational frameworks in English. In K. Aijmer & B. Altenberg (Eds.), *English corpus linguistics: Studies in honour of Jan Svartvik* (pp. 128–143). Longman.
Schmitt, N. (2000). *Vocabulary in language teaching*. Cambridge University Press.
Scott, M. (2004). *Oxford Word Smith tools 4.0 manual*. Oxford University Press.
Shi, C. (2013). Construction view in sentence analysis and related theoretical issues. *Chinese Linguistics, 2*, 23–38.
Shi, C. (2014). Recruitment" and "job application": Bidirectional interaction in construction suppression mechanism. *Contemporary Rhetoric, 2*, 1–11.
Stubbs, M. (2002). Two quantitative methods of studying phraseology in English. *International Journal of Corpus Linguistics, 2*, 215–244.
Su, D., & Lu, J. (2010). Syntax analysis method and teaching method of "construction-chunk." *Chinese Teaching in the World, 4*, 557–567.

Sun, H., & Yu, S. (2000). Overview of shallow syntactic methods. *Contemporary Linguistics, 2,* 74–83.

Wang, J. (2012). Experimental study on chunk teaching strategies to improve accuracy in student conference interpreting. *Chinese Translators Journal, 2,* 47–51.

Wang, L., & Chen, X. (2009). Progress of language chunk teaching and research in China—Review of "first national academic symposium on language chunk teaching and research". *Journal of Shanghai International Studies University, 6,* 90–94.

Wang, L., & Chen, X. (2012). *Theoretical and empirical progress in language chunk.* Shanghai Foreign Language Education Press.

Wang, W., & Huang, Y. (2013). Empirical study on the relationship between lexical chunk use and interpreting output. *Journal of Yangzhou University (Humanities and Social Sciences Edition), 4,* 28–35.

Wang, L., & Qian, J. (2009). Lexical chunk features in Chinese students' English speeches: An investigation based on corpus. *Foreign Language Research, 2,* 115–120.

Wang, L., & Zhang, D. (2006). Research progress on second language prefabricated chunk acquisition abroad. *Foreign Languages and Their Teaching, 5,* 17–21.

Watanabe, T., Sumit, E., & Okuno, H. G. (2003). Chunk-based statistical translation. In E. W. Hinrichs & D. Roth (Eds.), *Proceedings of the 41st Annual Meeting of the Association for Computational Linguistics* (pp. 303–310). Association for Computational Linguistics.

Wei, N. (2004). Preliminary study on oral corpus of Chinese English learners. *Modern Foreign Languages, 2,* 140–149.

Widdowson, H. G. (1989). Knowledge of language and ability for use. *Applied Linguistics, 10,* 128–137.

Widdowson, H. G. (1999). *Aspects of language teaching.* Shanghai Foreign Language Education Press.

Wong-Fillmore, L. (1976). *The second time around: Cognitive and social strategies in second language acquisition.* Doctoral dissertation, Stanford University.

Wray, A. (2000). Formulaic sequences in second language teaching: Principle and practice. *Applied Linguistics, 21*(4), 463–489.

Wray, A. (2002). *Formulaic language and the lexicon.* Cambridge University Press.

Xue, X. (2013). Review of conceptual representation and cognitive definition of English chunks. *Journal of Xi'an Foreign Languages University, 2,* 23–27.

Xue, X., & Shi, C. (2013). Nature and hierarchical relationship of lexical chunks in Chinese lexical chunk system. *Contemporary Rhetoric, 3,* 32–46.

Xu, Q. (2010). Chunks from the perspective of foreign language teaching: Development and issues. *Foreign Languages in China, 2,* 75–79.

Xu, J., & Xu, Z. (2007). Interactive discourse chunk study in Chinese students' oral English. *Foreign Language Teaching and Research, 6,* 437–443.

Yan, W. (2003). Role of chunks in basic vocabulary acquisition. *Journal of PLA University of Foreign Languages, 6,* 58–62.

Yan, C. (2006). Introduction to constructional grammar. *Journal of PLA University of Foreign Languages, 4,* 6–11.

Yang, Y. (1999). Block" nature of English vocabulary and its implications for English teaching. *Foreign Language World, 3,* 24–26.

Yuan, Z. (2009). Role and implications of chunks in translation process. *Foreign Language World, 5,* 83–89.

Yuan, P., & Guo, F. (2010). Correlation study on lexical chunks and fluency in second language oral speech. *Foreign Language World, 1,* 54–62.

Zhan, H. (2011). Tools and methods for extracting chunks from corpus. *Foreign Language Teaching, 2,* 23–26.

Zhang, L. (2001). Prefabricated chunks" and written discourse. *Journal of Inner Mongolia Normal University (Social Sciences), 4,* 84–87.

Zhang, F. (2013). *Use and functional analysis of lexical chunks in business English letters*. Master's thesis, Harbin Institute of Technology.
Zhang, J. (2013). Ten years of research on Chinese constructional grammar. *Chinese Language Learning, 5*, 65–76.
Zhang, C., Li, S., & Zhao, T. (2006). Phrase alignment based on central chunk extension. *Journal of Computer Research and Development, 9*, 1658–1665.
Zhou, J. (2007). Value and function of chunks in teaching Chinese as a foreign language. *Jinan Journal (Philosophy & Social Sciences), 1*, 99–103.
Zhou, Q. (2007). Basic block description system of Chinese. *Journal of Chinese Information Processing, 3*, 21–27.
Zhou, Q. (2008). Automatic learning and extension of basic block rules in Chinese. *Journal of Tsinghua University (Philosophy and Social Sciences), 1*, 88–91.
Zhou, Z. (2010). Research on linguistic features and applications of business English letters from the dimension of "chunks." *Journal of Hunan First Normal University, 4*, 123–126.
Zhou, Z., & Liao, C. (2008). Lexical chunk teaching method and its application in teaching business English letters. *Journal of Shenyang University (Social Sciences Edition), 3*, 33–36.
Zhou, Q., Zhan, W., & Ren, H. (2001). Construction of large-scale Chinese chunk library. In C. Huang & P. Zhang (Eds.), *Natural language understanding and machine translation* (pp. 102–107). Tsinghua University Press.
Zhou, Y., Zong, C., & Xu, B. (2005). Statistical machine translation based on multi-level filtering. *Journal of Chinese Information Processing, 3*, 54–60.
Zhu, Y. (2012). Critical reflections on lexical chunk studies. *Journal of Yangzhou University (Humanities and Social Sciences Edition), 1*, 124–128.

Chapter 2
MT-Oriented Analysis of Chunk Composition in Business Correspondences

2.1 Introduction

This chapter gives an MT-oriented analysis of chunk composition in business English letters, which mainly examines the relationship between chunks and constructions from the perspective of construction grammar, in an attempt to propose a theoretical model for chunk composition and to discuss the definition and criteria of chunks in business English letters in MT, providing theoretical support for related studies. The book mainly relies on a self-built English-Chinese parallel corpus of business correspondences with a total of about 1 million words, providing a rich resource for the MT-oriented study of corresponding lexical chunks in business correspondences from English to Chinese.

2.2 Theoretical Model of Chunk Composition Analysis

Instead of trying developing a specific study within the framework of construction grammar, this book analyzes the relationship between chunks and constructions with the help of insights obtained from certain properties of constructions, providing theoretical support for the MT-oriented study of corresponding lexical chunks in business correspondences from English to Chinese. Based on the literature review, the connotation of "construction" is quite consistent with the chunk theory and the construction grammar theory. However, since the basic goals and processing strategies of chunks and constructions are different, the basic nature and extension of the two concepts are inevitably both similar and essentially different. From their relationship, we could better understand the composition of chunks have a better understanding of their relations.

As a relatively fixed structure composed of multiple word units, lexical chunk is proposed in linguistic research. However, due to the different research backgrounds,

F. Hu, *An MT-Oriented Study of Corresponding Lexical Chunks in Business Correspondences from English to Chinese*,
https://doi.org/10.1007/978-981-99-4977-9_2

purposes, perspectives and methods, there is a huge divergence in understanding its connotation, properties, types as well as inner systemic nature in the academic community. At present, the research scope of chunks is gradually expanding, and the classification is becoming more and more detailed, which inevitably will bring new problems. Since systematically research on related phenomena and description of related concepts in terms of information processing units and form and pairing of form and meaning have not been attempted before, which could be rather chaotic, it needs to be put under the framework of construction grammar.

Understanding the nature of chunks often involves how to recognize the relationship between chunks and constructions, which, if accurately mastered, will be conducive to further delineating the internal relationship of the chunk system. This book makes an attempt to clarify the nature of chunks by drawing on the basic concepts of construction grammar and chunk theory, so as to lay a foundation for MT-oriented chunk analysis of business English correspondence.

In recent years, Lu Jianming and Su Danjie have proposed the construction-chunk approach (Lu, 2011a, 2011b, 2012a; Su, 2010, 2011, 2012a, 2012b, 2012c; Su & Lu, 2010; Xue & Shi, 2013), and have discussed the relations between constructions and chunks based on the thoughts of research methods in parsing. Obtained from the fruits, they have begun the combination of construction and chunk teaching, which is of high practical significance. On May 16–17, 2009, the author attended the First National Symposium on Formulaic Sequence Teaching and Research which was held at the School of International Studies of the University of International Business and Economics. In the keynote speech, Lu Jianming gave a presentation entitled "See Lexical Chunks in the Light of Constructions", arguing that "constructions and chunks may rewrite the history of Chinese grammar" (Wang & Chen, 2012). Lu (2012b) further discusses the multiplicity of semantic structural relations among the same words, prompting to find new analytical tools for sentence structures that are difficult to interpret through traditional ideas and methods. In teaching Chinese as a foreign language, Su Danjie encountered problems when interpreting certain sentence structures (such as existential sentences, partitive sentences, etc.) in traditional ways, which motivates Su to seek new analytical approaches. Above scholars both adopt coincidentally draw on the theory of construction grammar and gradually develop the construction-chunk approach. Su (2012c) points out that this approach is a syntactic-semantic analysis method based on construction grammar and chunks, and the basic idea is that there are various constructions at the syntactic level of language.

According to Su and Lu (2010), the core of chunks is that, the maximum number of discrete chunks that the brain can accommodate for both coding and decoding is "7 ± 2", supported by psychological experiments. Thus, an utterance is ostensibly composed of morphemes or words, but the actual constituent in the processing is a chunk. Su (2012c) also states that what they mean by "chunks" is neither defined by internal constituents, nor lexical chunks or formulaic language, which occur frequently at the lexical level and have a certain idiomaticity in current foreign language teaching. The "chunk" in construction-chunk approach is viewed from the perspective of constructions, and is top-down defined in terms of the semantic configuration of the constructions. Therefore, it refers to the lexical component of a construction that assumes a relatively independent part of the semantic unit. The combination of construction theory and chunk theory gives insights to the construction-chunk approach.

Actually, the construction-chunk approach is a usage-based view of grammar, in line with Croft and Cruse's (2004) view that the relationship between the parts within a construction must be semantically defined. This approach is concerned with and explores how language expresses the meaning of a cognitive concept in the form of a construction, and how the meaning of a construction is expressed in the form of a chunk chain. It focuses on what and why are these constructions at the syntactic level of language. According to Su (2012c), in terms of sentence constructions, the generality and individuality of languages are mainly reflected in the similarity and difference of chunk chains, which refer to the number, nature, order of chunks, as well as the grammatical means within chunks.

However, Shi (2011) holds the view that the understanding of the core concepts of chunks and constructions in theoretical studies is different from that in general chunk and construction theory. Xue and Shi (2013) further point out that a chunk in general chunk theory is a prefabricated structure as a unit of information processing in communication, a linguistic structural unit between word and syntax in the conventional sense. As a unit of information communication, limited recursiveness or even the absence of recursiveness is the basic external requirement for a chunk. Technically, although a lexical chunk is a type of chunks, in the context of contemporary language research and in the actual interpretation of Su (2012c), perhaps the "construction-chunk" approach here should be understood as a "sentence-chunk" approach in essence. At the same time, Lu (2011a) emphasizes that the construction-chunk approach is not mature yet, lacking basic research. It is not to be completely dismissive of the traditional syntactic analysis and grammar teaching, but to be free from the traditional syntactic analysis, because no syntactic analysis or method can be used for all purposes.

Based on the construction grammar and chunks, this chapter proposes a theoretical model of chunk composition analysis, presenting the relation between construction, chunk and word as a triangular as shown in Fig. 2.1.

Fig. 2.1 Theoretical model of chunk composition analysis

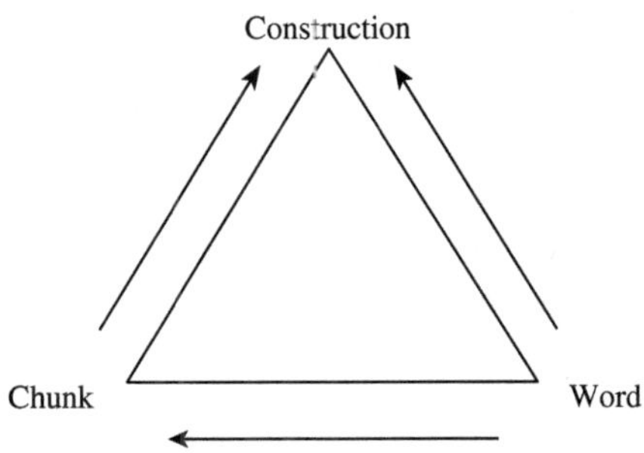

The classical definition of a construction given by Goldberg (1995) is that "C is a CONSTRUCTION iff def C is a form-meaning pair such that some aspects of Fi or some aspects of Si is not strictly predictable from C's components parts or from other previously established constructions." Later, construction grammar further extends "form-meaning pairs" to "form and meaning/function pairs" (Goldberg, 2003, 2006) where function includes meaning and usage. Thus, any linguistic unit that is a combination of form and meaning/function can be regarded as a construction. According to Han (2002), one can solve more than 99% of the problems in communication by mastering 5000 common words in a target language. Howarth (1998) argues that native speakers are fluent in their own language mainly owing to their mastery of lexical chunks. Lu (2005) suggests that the unit of sentence order should be the chunk rather than the word, and that the order within a sentence should be the "chunk sequence" while the order within a chunk is supposed to be the "word order". Lu (2012a) argues that chunks should be learned from the perspective of constructions. In this way, the chunk is an integral part of constructions, acting as a constituent of constructions, which is supported by Wang and Chen (2009), explaining that chunk can be seen as an organic component of constructions, in order to promote the second language teaching, especially in Chinese information processing. Chunks are prefabricated in memory, which will be extracted as a whole in a specific communicative situation and processed in combination as needed by the speaker, ensuring the semantic integrity and increasing the speed of language output, thus achieving the unity of accuracy and fluency. The features of constructions are the fundamental embodiments of the specific communicative function of chunks. In this regard, chunks are the main components of constructions. According to Yan (2006), a construction, in a broad sense, is still "a pairing of form and meaning and function". He classifies constructions into substantive constructions and schematic constructions, the former is lexically fixed with only one instance while the latter referring to more than semi-fixed phrases with more than one instance. In this chapter, constructions are considered to be composed of words and chunks respectively. Chunks are formed by words, and act as the main constituent of constructions. MT-oriented chunks in business correspondences refer to those concrete communicative components that exist as substantive "chunks", and words and smaller units (morphemes) and abstract structural rules are excluded. Therefore, an MT-oriented chunk in business correspondences is a substantive construction, which is a pairing of form and meaning/function.

Construction grammar provides a new perspective, requiring theoretical support for case studies and an effective systematic approach. Since we are still in the exploratory stage, the analysis methods that have been adopted need to be improved, and we hope more researchers venture into the analysis methods that are applicable to construction grammar.

2.3 MT-Oriented Definition of Chunks in Business English Correspondences

According to Wray (2008), the definition of chunks is closely related to the research purpose. The study aims to provide theoretical support and basic resources for the development of MT-oriented English-Chinese business letter corresponding chunk banks, which is also the starting point for the definition of chunks. Therefore, this chapter defines the business English corresponding chunks for MT as follows:

The "MT-oriented chunk in business correspondences" is a substantive construction, i.e., a pairing of form and meaning/function, an essentially unambiguous, highly reusable, individual and continuous multi-word unit as a whole.

This research need to be integrated in a complementary manner according to the following criteria.

A. A substantive construction, i.e., a pairing of form and meaning/function

According to the construction grammar, a chunk is a major construction. Constructions exist at different levels of the language, which could be considered as constructions as long as they are a pairing of form and meaning/function. In business English letters, a chunk is characterized by the meaning-form combination and coding extraction as a whole, making it a good construction. MT-oriented chunks in business correspondences refer to those concrete communicative components that exist as substantive "chunks" which are also combinations of form and meaning/function.

B. Basically no ambiguity

Context always activates the appropriate meaning of ambiguous words, and the paradigm of chunks and the contextual information matching determine the low frequency of the chunk ambiguity. Therefore, the chunk that has become formulaic language is of great value in context. The richness of the chunk information and the contextual information matching determine the affluence of the semantic links and the narrowing of the semantic category search space, making it easier for people to quickly recall and ensure that they are quickly understood and extracted in a certain context, greatly improving the richness of the subject's linguistic expressions, and also enhancing the authenticity (Li et al., 2012).

The business English letter chunks are created and gradually fixed in use, i.e., they undergo the process of chunking (often composed of free combination). But as an immediate information processing unit, they are a combination of form and meaning/function. In order to achieve the effect of "one chunk representing one meaning" and exclude the ambiguity in MT, the principle of extension priority must be followed when analyzing the bilingual chunk correspondence, that is, when merging or splitting chunks, the merging method should be given priority. However, the property of "no ambiguity" can hardly be guaranteed in the real sense. A very small number of bilingual corresponding chunks may be free of ambiguity in the original context, but ambiguity may still arise in the target language if without specific context. Therefore, this property is conveyed as "basically no ambiguity".

C. High degree of reuse

The degree of reuse describes, in a translation unit, the correspondence between the source language unit and its counterpart in target language in various contexts, which is influenced by extratextual and intratextual factors (Su & Ding, 2009). The degree of reuse is a decisive factor in determining whether a linguistic combination unit is a lexical chunk or not. Therefore, in determining whether a linguistic combination unit is a chunk, it is necessary to see whether it is frequently used together. If the degree of reuse is high, it could be identified as a chunk.

D. Individual whole units

From the achievements in psycholinguistics, cognitive linguistics, corpus linguistics, and others, it can be seen that chunks, as linguistic units stored and extracted as a whole, can reduce the difficulty in linguistic information processing. MT-oriented chunks in business correspondences are obtained as a whole, and entirely stored in the MT case library as an example, with more fixed grammatical structure and more stable meaning collocation. They are extracted as a whole when needed, ensuring the semantic integrity and improving the translation speed at the same time.

E. Multi-word units

Chunks in business correspondences are usually larger than two words and smaller than nine words. In MT, chunks less than nine words are the appropriate granularity units for translation matching.

2.4 Corpus Data

Parallel corpus is an important tool and resource for language comparison and MT research, and has far-reaching significance for the development of bilingual information retrieval and MT systems. There are unidirectional and bidirectional parallel corpus, the former containing texts in source and target languages while the latter containing an original text translated into the target language and vice versa. Meanwhile, the parallel corpus can be either bilingual or multilingual (Olohan, 2004). A bilingual parallel corpus consists of texts in both source and target languages, and usually different levels of alignment are established between the texts according to the translation relationship (Chang, 2006). The construction of a parallel corpus uses computer alignment to connect the original text with the translation at the level of words, sentences or paragraphs. Therefore, the development of different levels of alignment is critical. Alignment is not only a key aspect of case library construction in MT, but also a necessary prerequisite for acquiring linguistic knowledge and conducting comparative word studies based on corpus (Li & Zhao, 2013). The parallel corpus covered in this chapter consists of the original text and its corresponding translations, i.e. the word "parallel" is understood as a translation correspondence, which contains discourse, paragraph, sentence, and word.

At present, many parallel corpora have been built at home and abroad, and a brief introduction is given as follows. The first parallel corpus built abroad is the Canadian Hansards Corpus, which collects 50 million words of official records of Canadian parliamentary sessions. Mainly in the legal field, the data covers topics such as impromptu discussions, written materials, and prepared speeches, composed of T Treebank, LDC, and the TransSearch Corpus. The English-Norwegian parallel corpus at the University of Oslo contains mainly fiction and non-fiction texts, with lexical annotation of the English parts by the researcher, and is mainly used for applied linguistic and theoretical linguistic studies. The Chemnitz E–G Translation Corpus project is a bilingual, bi-directional parallel corpus with English and German as source texts and corresponding target texts respectively, ranging from contemporary English and American literature to science textbooks. The aim of the corpus is to create a machine-readable and aligned corpus to discover and categorize translation counterparts of linguistic items such as prepositions, functional verbs, demonstratives, metaphors and culture-loaded words and expressions. Results of the study are applied to bilingual lexicography, language teaching and MT.

Domestically, the most influential is the Chinese English-Chinese Parallel Corpus developed by Wang Kefei of the National Research Centre for Foreign Language Education of Beijing Foreign Studies University, supported by the Major Project Fund of the Key Research Bases of Humanities and Social Sciences of the Ministry of Education and the Major Project Fund of the National Social Sciences. It is the largest English-Chinese parallel corpus at present,[1] including literature, news, political, scientific and technical, and application texts, totaling about 100 million words (50 million words in the general English-Chinese parallel corpus and over 50 million words in the specialized English-Chinese parallel corpus). A representative parallel corpus designed for MT is the Chinese-English Bilingual Aligned Corpus jointly developed by the Institute of Computational Linguistics of Peking University in China, the National Key Laboratory of Intelligent Technology and Systems of Tsinghua University and the Institute of Computing Technology of the Chinese Academy of Sciences. It is designed for a sub-project of the National Key Basic Research Project (973) "Chinese-English Machine Translation System for Journalism" hosted by Yu Shiwen of the Institute of Computational Linguistics of Peking University. The data comes from news, government documents, and scientific and technical literature. The group has also developed a Chinese-English bilingual phrase database with the aim of improving the translation quality of rule-based translation systems. Furthermore, the Chinese-English bilingual corpus developed by the Hong Kong University of Science and Technology mainly collects and processes the minutes of the Legislative Council of the Hong Kong Special Administrative Region, including the Chinese-English bilingual court judgments.

[1] As of April 2014, 90% of the corpus has been completed. For details, please refer to the mid-term inspection report of "Establishment and Processing of a Super-large-scale English-Chinese Parallel Corpus" published on the website of the National Office for Philosophy and Social Sciences http://www.npopss-cn.gov.cn/n/2014/0226/c373521-24473983.html [2014-04-22].

The parallel corpus can quickly analyze a large number of bilingual aligned corpora, providing translation examples for example-based MT engines and improving the quality of translation. The bilingual aligned corpus also provides a basic resource for exploring various MT knowledge, for instance, translation knowledge of chunks obtained from the bilingual aligned corpus. Therefore, building a bilingual parallel corpus will be conducive to strengthening the automatic processing capability of MT and increasing the translation accuracy.

Since 2009, the author has hosted a youth fund project "Research on the extraction of chunk based on English-Chinese business correspondence corpus" (2009QR04) of the university, a key project of Luoyang social science "Research on parallel corpus and English-Chinese business correspondence translation" (2013A042) and a project of Henan Science and Technology Department "Development of English-Chinese business correspondence parallel corpus" (132400410949). Funded by these projects, a bilingual corpus of English-Chinese business correspondences with a size of about 2 million words has been successfully built, including four sub-corpora: English business correspondence corpus, Chinese business correspondence corpus, English-Chinese business correspondence parallel corpus, and Chinese-English business correspondence parallel corpus. On this basis, a parallel English-Chinese business correspondence corpus with a size of about 1 million words is further constructed and processed, which provides a solid foundation for the study of English-Chinese business correspondence corresponding chunks for MT.

Business correspondences contain thank you letters and sale letters. The former is used frequently in business communication to contact feelings, enhance friendship and promote trade, including letters of thanks, congratulations, condolences and invitations related to business transactions; the latter serves for contacting business, negotiating cooperation and solving economic problems, including letters of cooperation intention, promotion, credit inquiry, inquiry, offer and counter offer, purchase, shipment, payment, claim and insurance, which cover the whole process of business activities. In terms of formality, business entertainment letters can also be called memorandums because they deal with general or courtesy matters and are shorter in length; business operation letters can also be called formal letters, which are generally longer in length, complete in structure and clear in content and deal with concrete business matters (Zhang & Li, 2003). The data of the English-Chinese business correspondence parallel corpus is mainly classified as follows:

(1) Letters of cooperation intention. Letters of cooperation intention mainly introduce how to obtain information about the other company and express the desire to establish business relationship, in which you can introduce the nature and scope of your business, or offer your product catalog.
(2) Letters of promotion, aiming to arouse the interest of the other party to buy products or services. At the same time, the advantages of your products and various preferential conditions should be consciously highlighted. At the end, try to use clever expression to motivate the other party to order, such as possible rise in price, limited stock, discounts on large orders, and free trials.

(3) Letters of credit inquiry. This type refers to the seller's inquiry into the buyer's creditworthiness and business ability through certain means, and the seller could request the buyer to provide credit information to examine creditworthiness.
(4) Letters of inquiry. The purpose is to ask the other party to provide information about products and services, such as catalogs, price lists, samples, quotations, etc.
(5) Letters of offer and counter offer. Making an offer to the other party is usually accompanied by a quotation, including the description of the goods, the quantity available, commodity specifications, packaging conditions, unit price, payment method, delivery date and expiration date. If the buyer accepts the offer, he will make an agreement. If not, he will propose a modification to the terms of the offer, which is called a counter offer. If the seller does not agree with the modifications and then proposes new conditions, it is called a counter-counter offer.
(6) Letters of purchase, common letters for the purchase of goods or services. After the buyer receives the letter of offer, if he thinks the goods and prices are suitable, and determines to purchase, he will write a formal order to the seller, which is the letter of purchase. It should be clearly about the name, number, specification, quantity, price, shipment, delivery date, payment conditions, packaging, insurance and other matters.
(7) Letters of shipment. When the two sides reach a deal, the seller will ship the goods to the other party within the specified period in accordance with the contract. Once the goods are loaded on the ship, vehicle or plane, the seller shall notify the buyer by way of a letter stating the order number or contract number of the batch of goods, and attaching the bill of lading, invoice, inspection certificate, weight list, and insurance policy so that the buyer can handle the procedures of picking up and paying for the goods.
(8) Letters of payment. After the buyer receives the goods, payment matters should be handled. Payment methods basically include remittance, collection and letter of credit. No matter which one is adopted, the buyer should notify the seller of the payment method and process in the form of a letter.
(9) Letters of claim. Letters of claim come from one party to a transaction who has suffered a loss in trading to the other party requesting compensation. The letter of claim consists of three parts: a statement of the original terms of the contract, a description of the breach of the contract, and an offer of compensation for the loss.
(10) Letters of insurance. In order to ensure a timely compensation after suffering losses, the parties concerned will purchase insurance for the goods in accordance with the transportation, the nature of the goods and the provisions of the contract. The cargo owner could apply for the appropriate insurance in terms of the content and terms, fill out the policy, and provide factors affecting the conditions of insurance. The insurance company performs its duties after underwriting and compensates the insured according to the relevant agreement in a timely manner after loss.

According to Maia (2003), four types of texts are not suitable for the translation research corpus, including: (1) the original text may itself be a translation, or written by an author with limited competence in the source language; (2) the translation may have been done in a hurry, and consequently contain errors or reflect the textual and syntactic structure of the original too closely; (3) the translation may have been done by a non-native speaker of the target language, or by a native-speaker without training in translation; (4) the original and/or the translation may have been subjected to editorial interference, not always beneficially. In building a parallel corpus of English-Chinese business correspondences, the following basic principles are proposed in this chapter: (1) the selected corpus should be of high translation quality, mainly the business correspondence textbooks published by authoritative publishers; (2) the classification of the corpus should be clear, mainly 10 types: letters of cooperation intention, promotion, credit inquiry, inquiry, offer and counter offer, purchase, shipment, payment, claim and insurance in the whole business activities; (3) with the help of natural language processing tools and human resources, the alignment at the discourse and sentence level will be realized.

2.5 Summary

Through the integration of multiple disciplines, there will be less controversy about the effectiveness of chunks, and its positioning in linguistics will move in an increasingly rational direction (Li, 2011). The chunk is the main construction, referring to those concrete communicative components that exist as substantive "chunks", and words and smaller units (morphemes) and abstract structural rules are excluded. Some scholars even consider discourse as a kind of chunk. However, in actual communication, children's songs and religious scriptures are seldom used as units of information processing, making it of little significance to be included in the study of chunks (Xue & Shi, 2013). A theoretical model of chunk composition is proposed and the definition of MT-oriented chunks in business English correspondences is given in this chapter. The definition provides theoretical support for related studies. Meanwhile, this chapter also introduces the English-Chinese business correspondence parallel corpus, providing an important basic resource for chunk extraction in business English correspondences in Chap. 3.

References

Chang, B. (2006). A bilingual dictionary compilation platform based on corpus. *Lexicographical Studies, 3*, 122–133.

Croft, W., & Cruse, D. A. (2004). *Cognitive linguistics*. Cambridge University Press.

Goldberg, E. (1995). *Constructions: A construction grammar approach to argument structure*. The University of Chicago Press.

Goldberg, E. (2003). Constructions: A new theoretical approach to language. *Journal of Foreign Languages, 3*, 1–11.
Goldberg, E. (2006). *Constructions at work*. Oxford University Press.
Han, B. (2002). *Language and human meaning*. China Social Sciences Press.
Howarth, P. (1998). Phraseology and second language proficiency. *Applied Linguistics, 19*(1), 24–44.
Li, J. (2011). Review of domestic and foreign chunk studies. *Shandong Foreign Language Teaching, 5*, 17–23.
Li, J., Li, L., & Gao, X. (2012). Lexical chunk research from the perspective of hermeneutics. *Foreign Language Research, 6*, 74–78.
Li, J., & Zhao, X. (2013). Research on recognition and application of corresponding word sequences in parallel texts. *Technology Enhanced Foreign Languages, 5*, 36–40.
Lu, C. (2005). Cognitive study on the modern Chinese word order from the perspective of expectation theory. *Chinese Teaching in the World, 1*, 32–43.
Lu, J. (2011a). Revisiting construction chunk analysis method. *Studies in Language and Linguistics, 2*, 1–7.
Lu, J. (2011b). Language studies need continuous exploration and innovation: Three examples from English-Chinese contrast. *Journal of PLA University of Foreign Languages, 4*, 1–6.
Lu, J. (2012a). Lexical chunk analysis from the perspective of construction. In L. Wang & X. Chen (Eds.), *Theoretical and empirical progress in language chunk* (pp. 43–50). Shanghai Foreign Language Education Press.
Lu, J. (2012b). Re-discussion on the multiple relationships in semantic structures between identical words. *Journal of Soochow University (Philosophy and Social Science Edition), 4*, 5–11.
Maia, B. (2003). Some languages are more equal than others: Training translators in terminology and information retrieval using comparable and parallel corpora. In F. Zanettin, S. Bernardini, & D. Stewart (Eds.), *Corpora in translator education* (pp. 43–53). St. Jerome.
Olohan, M. (2004). *Introducing corpora in translation studies*. Routledge Taylor & Francis Group.
Shi, C. (2011). Basic status and research orientation of Chinese construction study for second language teaching. *Language Teaching and Linguistic Studies, 6*, 98–108.
Su, D. (2010). Analysis of "construction-chunk" teaching method—Taking existential sentences teaching and experiment as an example. *Chinese Language Learning, 2*, 83–90.
Su, D. (2011). Essence of construction-chunk teaching method—Taking ditransitive sentence teaching and experiment as an example. *Language Teaching and Linguistic Studies, 2*, 16–22.
Su, D. (2012a). Chunk as an intermediate between construction and lexeme—Taking modern Chinese "V-Qi NP Lai" as an example. *Journal of Sun Yatsen University (Social Science Edition), 1*, 69–77.
Su, D. (2012b). Abolishing the notion of "ditransitive sentence"—New analysis of construction-chunk method. *Studies in Language and Linguistics, 2*, 100–107.
Su, D. (2012c). Construction is a chain of lexical chunks—Theoretical framework of construction-chunk analysis method. *Linguistic Sciences, 3*, 241–253.
Su, M., & Ding, S. (2009). Implications of translation unit research for computer-assisted translation. *Foreign Languages Research, 6*, 84–89.
Su, D., & Lu, J. (2010). Syntax analysis method and teaching method of "construction-chunk." *Chinese Teaching in the World, 4*, 557–567.
Wang, L., & Chen, X. (2009). Progress of language chunk teaching and research in China—Review of "First national academic symposium on language chunk teaching and research". *Journal of Shanghai International Studies University, 6*, 90–94.
Wang, L., & Chen, X. (2012). *Theoretical and empirical progress in language chunk*. Shanghai Foreign Language Education Press.
Wray, A. (2008). *Formulaic Language: Pushing the boundaries*. Oxford University Press.
Xue, X., & Shi, C. (2013). Nature and hierarchical relationship of lexical chunks in Chinese lexical chunk system. *Contemporary Rhetoric, 3*, 32–46

Yan, C. (2006). Introduction to constructional grammar. *Journal of PLA University of Foreign Languages, 4*, 6–11.
Zhang, X., & Li, M. (2003). *Business English translation*. Higher Education Press.

Chapter 3
Chunk Extraction in Business English Correspondences

3.1 Introduction

At present, no scholars have conducted MT-oriented research on the chunk extraction of human–computer interaction in business English correspondences. This chapter proposes to conduct a study on the extraction of business English corresponding chunks through three modules: text pre-processing, automatic extraction and manual processing, focusing on the automatic computer extraction of two to nine words according to the definition and definition criteria of MT-oriented business English corresponding chunks. With the corpus chunk extraction software, the computerized automatic extraction of chunks from the English-Chinese parallel business correspondence corpus is carried out, and then the chunks that do not meet the definition manually are removed to obtain the table of MT-oriented business English letter chunks. This study probes into a key technology for an MT-oriented English-Chinese business letter corresponding chunk bank.

3.2 Text Preprocessing Module

In this chapter, ABBYY Aligner, automatic alignment software, is applied to the parallel corpus of English-Chinese business letters alignment at both the discourse and sentence levels, as shown in Figs. 3.1 and 3.2.

Due to the limited time and manpower, 400 business letters in English and 400 business letters in Chinese (115,026 words in total, about one-tenth of the corpus, including 46,868 words in English and 68,158 single words in Chinese) were randomly selected from the English-Chinese parallel corpus of about 1 million words. The 400 English letters and the corresponding 400 Chinese letters are renamed as 1_E, 2_E, …, 400_E for English ones and 1_C, 2_C, …, 400_C for Chinese ones,

F. Hu, *An MT-Oriented Study of Corresponding Lexical Chunks in Business Correspondences from English to Chinese*,
https://doi.org/10.1007/978-981-99-4977-9_3

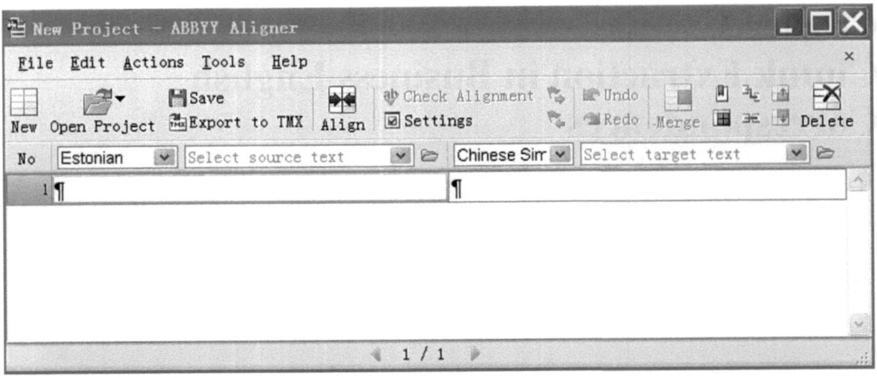

Fig. 3.1 ABBYY Aligner interface

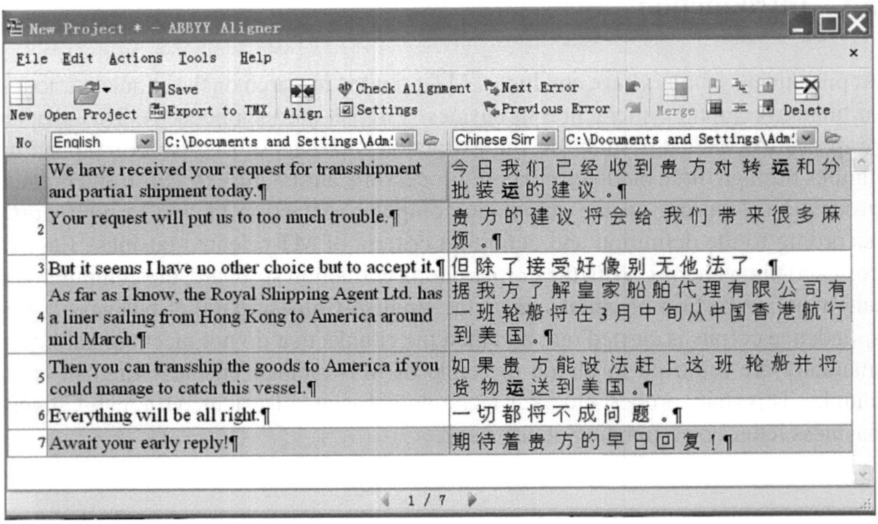

Fig. 3.2 Alignment screenshot of ABBYY aligner. *Note* Part of Chinese translations have been modified

with the format converted from TXT to UTF-8, as UTF-8 format is required for chunk extraction in a corpus.

3.3 Automatic Extraction Module

N-gram refers to a continuous word string consisting of two or more words, including dual structure, ternary structure, etc. (Zhan, 2011). Jiang Binggui and Zhang Qinlong from the Institute of Computational Linguistics of Peking University conducted a study on the automatic extraction of Chinese chunks for machine-assisted translation around 2007. They proposed a combined statistical and rule-based chunk extraction method, using Nagao string frequency statistical method to perform word-based string frequency and filtering 2–10 g chunks with statistical methods and chunk boundary handling rules to obtain candidate chunks with satisfactory results. Moreover, it is found that the combination of MI and information entropy is better than the single MI method; in chunk boundary handling rules, the chunk left and right boundary rules and the stop words have a great influence on chunk extraction. The experimental results show that the combination of statistics and handling rules is better than the pure statistical method. Supplemented by manual proofreading, we could easily obtain recurring chunks. In machine translation, by using the chunk extraction function to gain recurring linguistic units, translation memory and English-Chinese corresponding chunk banks can be conducted conveniently, thus to improve efficiency.

The research conducted by Jiang Binggui and others is of referential significance for this study. Although the chunk extraction techniques and the chunk banks are different, the basic principles are the same, i.e., in the MT system, chunk extraction is used to collect recurring linguistic units and build an English-Chinese corresponding chunk bank, so as to promote translation efficiency.

Based on information theory, MI is now used to measure the association strength or collocability between a node word and its collocates. University of Birmingham Language Centre has adopted a method for calculating MI values that is easily understood and widely accepted, which could be formalized as

$$\mathrm{MI}(x, y) = \frac{fabs.(x, y)}{f\mathrm{exp}.(x, y)}$$

where the head is expressed as x and collocate within a fixed length (4 words before and after the head) as y; observed co-occurrence frequency of the head as $f_{abs.}(x, y)$ and the expected co-occurrence frequency of the head and its collocates under the null hypothesis as $f_{\mathrm{exp.}}(x, y)$. The MI value reflects the extent to which the observed co-occurrence frequency is inconsistent with the expected, showing how much information is brought to the occurrence of y by that of x. Generally, the larger the MI value is, the greater the influence of x on the occurrence of y (Wang, 2006). Although the method of identifying the collocability in terms of MI value has certain drawbacks, it does provide language learners with intuitive and scientific collocation reference to a certain extent, enabling language educators and learners to grasp the semantic and collocation characteristics of a word easily and accurately when learning vocabulary (Feng & Wang, 1999).

In this chapter, 202,127 g were automatically extracted by the corpus phrase extraction system according to 2–9 g (inclusive), and 154,613 g were obtained after the de-emphasis as shown in Figs. 3.3 and 3.4. Among them, the Grams with MI value over 2 were extracted according to the frequency and then calculated through

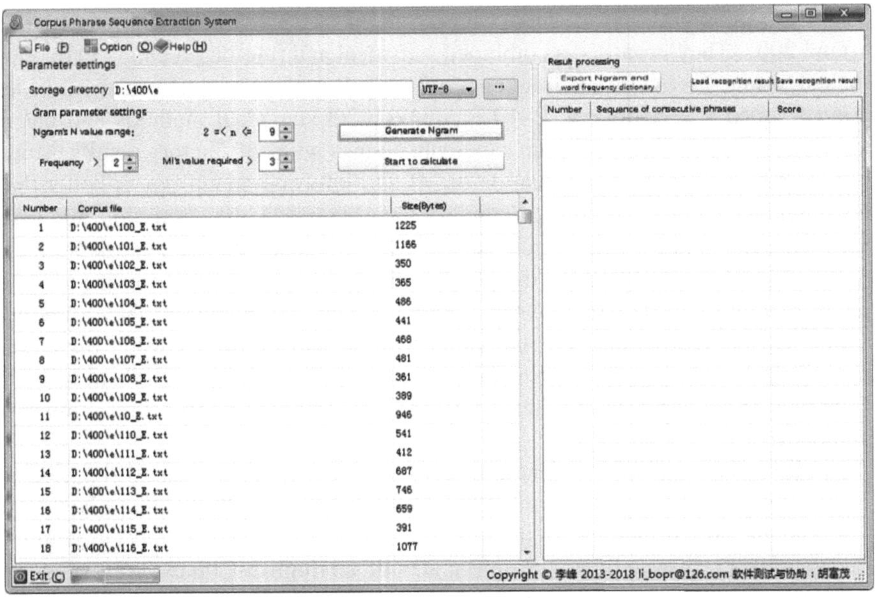

Fig. 3.3 Screenshot of the corpus phrase extraction system

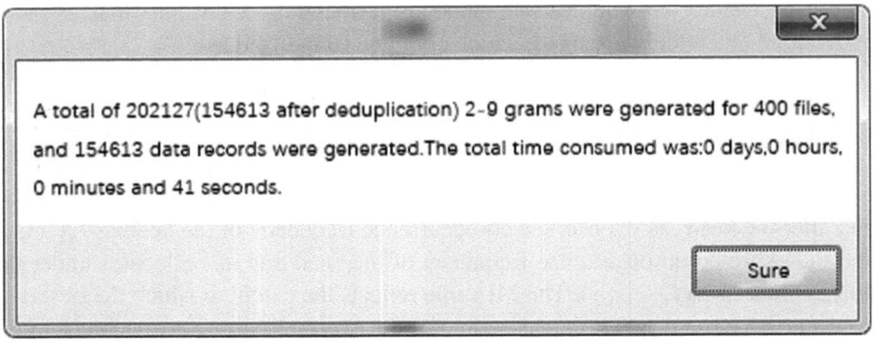

Fig. 3.4 Auto-generated results of 2–9 g in business English correspondences

the MI calculation to obtain 290 candidate chunks, and the final results were recorded in Word and Excel as shown in Appendix.[1]

The corpus phrase extraction system integrates big data application processing technologies, such as multi-CPU (central processing unit) parallel computing, concurrent multi-threading and MongoDB massive data storage under 64-bit platform to quickly grow N-gram sets within a specified range, and synchronously deduplicate and calculate the frequency of each Gram and of the left and right neighbors

[1] Candidate chunks (290), automatically extracted with words in lowercase after extraction (all words in the later tables are in lowercase), are sorted by original serial numbers for reference.

as well as neighboring words. The results are quickly stored in MongoDB through memory mapping to prepare for the next step. At the same time, the Grams containing obvious noise information such as punctuation and special characters are filtered to generate purer and more effective Grams set. Among clean sets of Grams, those appear only a few times, such as once or twice, are removed in terms of frequency as the threshold, and then the MI value are calculated by using the improved MI calculation in Wei and Li's (2013) study for the filtered results. After optimization for containing block, final chunks are obtained.

From Fig. 3.4, the following aspects need to be noted. First, the number of chunks drop from more than 200,000 g to more than 150,000 after the de-emphasis, which is not huge, mainly for two reasons: (1) as the length of Grams increases, the frequency becomes sparser, and many Grams appear only once, which cannot be eliminated in the de-emphasis process; (2) some conventional expressions repeat many times in business English correspondences, but the main contents are not the same to a large extent. Second, the frequency threshold is set over 2 instead of 1 for two reasons: (1) if the threshold is set too low, even if those Grams with a frequency of 2 are involved in calculation, they are too rare to be representative due to low absolute frequency, and the MI value may be low, which is not convincing and even meaningless; (2) a too low threshold is basically impossible and unacceptable in the industry, because the statistical calculation without statistical significance is also pointless.

A detailed left and right neighboring situation is shown in Fig. 3.5. The left and right neighboring structure of the process file: list of left words {"a": Freq.$_{(a)}$, "b": Freq.$_{(b)}$, ……}; list of right words {"a": Freq.$_{(a)}$, "b": Freq.$_{(b)}$, ……}.

The distribution of N values from 2 to 9 candidate chunks was obtained by counting 290 candidate chunks, as shown in Table 3.1.

Figure 3.6 provides a visual representation of the proportion of the 290 candidate chunks.

```
127413  your acceptance as soon as      5       1↓
                LeftWords: { "us" : 1 }↓
                RightWords: { "possible" : 1 }↓
↓
↓
127414  you can benefit a       4       1↓
                LeftWords: { "which" : 1 }↓
                RightWords: { "lot" : 1 }↓
↓
↓
127415  price is on rather      4       1↓
                LeftWords: { "your" : 1 }↓
                RightWords: { "high" : 1 }↓
```

Fig. 3.5 Screenshot of the sample structure in the N-gram procedure file

Table 3.1 Distribution of candidate chunks of N-Gram ($N = 2, 3, \ldots, 9$)

N	Number	Percentage (%)
2	81	27.93
3	55	18.97
4	52	17.93
5	30	10.34
6	31	10.69
7	15	5.17
8	16	5.52
9	10	3.45
Sum	290	100

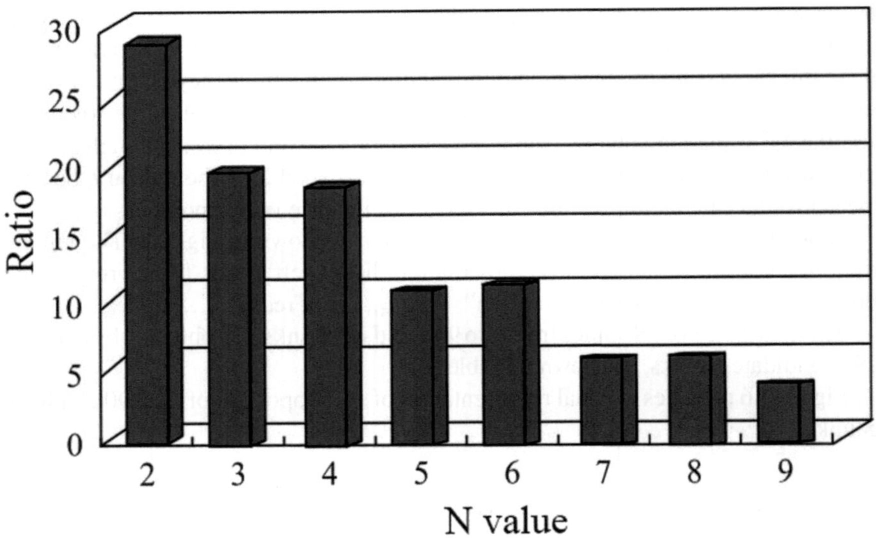

Fig. 3.6 Ratio of N in automatically extracted candidate chunks

Table 3.1 and Fig. 3.6 show that the number of candidate chunks when $N = 2$ is 81, or 27.93%, about one-third of the total; the sum of the candidate chunks when $N = 6$–9 is 72, or 24.83%, less than one-third; and there are 218 chunks with N values of 2–5, accounting for 75.17%, about three quarters of the total, proving the capacity limitation of 4 ± 1 items according to psychologist Nelson Cowan. When memorizing more than four discrete chunks, the difficulty increases sharply in processing the material behind. Therefore, when people memorize phone numbers in segments, each one will not exceed 3 or 4 digits. For example, a 10-digit number will be divided into three segments like 3–3–4 or 4–3–3, and never into the symmetrical 5–5 structure. This is because when remembering a five-digit segment, the ability to handle the following numbers is greatly reduced.

After counting the frequencies of the 290 chunks, a list of frequency in reverse order[2] was obtained, as shown in Table 3.2.

As shown in Table 3.2, the highest frequency of "thank you for your letter" is 43; the frequency of 10 or more is 16, accounting for 5.5%; the frequency of 6–9 is 17, occupying 5.9%, and the total proportion of the two is 11.4%. There were 21 chunks with a frequency of 5 (7.2%), 65 cases with a frequency of 4 (22.4%), and the sum of the two is 29.7%. The remaining is the frequency of 3 with 171 chunks, taking up 59.0%. Figure 3.7 is a pie chart of frequency.

The MI scores of 290 computer-automated candidate chunks of business English letters were obtained statistically. Due to the large quantity, only part of chunks (one-half of the total, i.e. 145) are presented as shown in Table 3.3.

By analyzing the MI scores and frequencies of the candidates, it is found that the highest MI score of "mutually beneficial" (7.024 871 426) has a frequency of 3. Among the ten candidates with MI scores above 6.0, all of them have a frequency of 3 except for the tenth one, which has a frequency of 4. However, "thank you for your letter" (43) has the highest MI score of 3.022 798 161, with the second lowest frequency. Among the eleven candidate chunks with a frequency of 10 or more, the MI score is below 5.0, except for "bill of lading" which is 5.455 707 412, verifying that the MI score and frequency are not correlated, and that other factors are needed to determine whether the candidates are genuine chunks, requires manual screening.

3.4 Manual Processing Module

Zhan (2011) points out that with certain criteria should be developed as a reference for judging in advance, automatic chunk identification needs human assistance in order to achieve complementary advantages. This chapter is based on the definition of an MT-oriented business English chunk, i.e., a substantive construction, a combination of form and meaning/function as well as a multi-word unit with essentially unambiguous nature and a high degree of reuse, which act as an individual whole unit.

For ease of operation, the specific criteria are: (i) a substantive construction, i.e., a combination of form and meaning/function; (ii) unambiguity; (iii) a high degree of reuse; (iv) individual whole units; and (v) multi-word units.

In addition, proper names, product-specific names and abbreviations should not be included because they are not seen as chunks in prevailing definitions and are easily found in general dictionaries and abbreviation dictionaries. The following is an analysis with N value as the standard of classification.

[2] The term "the reverse frequency list" is borrowed from the expression in *Translation Words from the Perspective of Thinking Modes* (published by Shanghai Foreign Language Education Press in 2012) by Feng Qinghua in the appendix.

Table 3.2 Reverse frequency list of automatically extracted candidate chunks

No.	Original serial number	Candidate chunks	Freq.
1	140133	thank you for your letter	43
2	154276	as soon as possible	26
3	124932	hong kong	18
4	115450	terms of payment	16
5	117474	sales confirmation	16
6	144232	new york	16
7	29315	pleased to inform	14
8	88255	look forward to your early reply	13
9	120779	irrevocable letter of credit	13
10	144216	upon receipt of	13
11	140614	terms and conditions	12
12	152860	bill of lading	12
13	83853	end of this month	11
14	116751	per dozen	11
15	50911	sole agency	10
16	58930	shipping documents	10
17	17093	at an early date	9
18	83754	shipping advice	8
19	140048	at the same time	8
20	47560	on going into the matter	7
21	115505	in the near future	7
22	139885	more than	7
23	140569	above address	7
24	144234	counter offer	7
25	3827	dear sir or madam	6
26	32170	good enough	6
27	103042	laser printer	6
28	104190	so that we can	6
29	105009	favorable reply	6
30	126626	valid until	6
31	128546	silk blouses	6
32	131380	large quantities	6
33	152019	formal agreement	6
34	17510	a wide range of	5
35	17529	be glad to learn	5
36	28936	in full settlement	5

(continued)

Table 3.2 (continued)

No.	Original serial number	Candidate chunks	Freq.
37	42553	prices we quoted	5
38	60086	comply with your request	5
39	74449	above mentioned	5
40	101838	please see to it that	5
41	102522	time of shipment	5
42	102695	by draft at sight	5
43	108547	usual practice	5
44	108879	good prospects	5
45	113157	other suppliers	5
46	115058	not later than	5
47	121457	prompt attention	5
48	125354	partial shipment	5
49	59930	regular customers	5
50	128580	brisk demand	5
51	130634	name and address	5
52	135671	want to know	5
53	137956	against all risks	5
54	149386	make this request	5
55	14440	past four years	4
56	16721	representative selection	4
57	17652	poor condition	4
58	21662	reach you in good time	4
59	23504	goods are shipped	4
60	23687	no available space	4
61	28885	cash discount	4
62	38557	entirely satisfactory	4
63	42463	special discount	4
64	53728	due to arrive	4
65	57451	sent herewith	4
66	57490	damaged during transit	4
67	57601	clean bill of lading	4
68	57658	claim to be lodged	4
69	57716	suggest you set out a claim immediately	4
70	57722	hope our explanation will be satisfactory	4
71	57732	a claim immediately against the shipping company	4
72	57754	have received your letter of april	4

(continued)

Table 3.2 (continued)

No.	Original serial number	Candidate chunks	Freq.
73	57781	good condition when they left here	4
74	57893	goods in question were carefully packed by experienced workmen	4
75	58084	unpacking the cases	4
76	58094	requirements of this market	4
77	58194	must return the goods to you	4
78	58199	look forward to your early settlement	4
79	58232	found that the quality was not satisfactory	4
80	58246	for the invoice value and inspection charges involved	4
81	58254	regret to inform you	4
82	58296	not up to the standard of samples	4
83	58298	the goods delivered is not up to the standard[3]	4
84	58328	too inferior to be suitable for the requirements	4
85	61364	dress materials supplied	4
86	61511	duly received the documents	4
87	66000	please let me know	4
88	77261	two years ago	4
89	79410	san francisco	4
90	81560	bank of china	4
91	82341	the people's insurance company of china	4
92	85611	debit note	4
93	88425	cotton sweaters	4
94	88878	under separate cover	4
95	89250	per hundred	4
96	91051	must stress	4
97	91356	thank you for your inquiry	4
98	93385	lower than	4
99	95582	packed in cartons	4
100	97377	keep dry	4
101	100362	thank you in advance for your cooperation	4
102	114413	may rest assured	4
103	114560	cfr basis	4
104	115471	latest catalogue	4
105	115506	within the next month	4
106	117192	drawn up	4

(continued)

[3] The original sentence is "The quality of the goods delivered is not up to the standard."

Table 3.2 (continued)

No.	Original serial number	Candidate chunks	Freq.
107	120629	ready for shipment	4
108	122272	selling season	4
109	123306	do your utmost to	4
110	123314	under the captioned contract	4
111	127043	on a cash basis	4
112	131387	electronic products	4
113	134170	plastic furniture	4
114	137039	window frames	4
115	143115	frying pan	4
116	144264	cif new york	4
117	144309	shipment to be made	4
118	149815	swimming trousers	4
119	152929	quite satisfactory	4

Note This table only presents the 119 candidates with a frequency of 4 or more; the other 171 candidates with the remaining chunks omitted due to space limitations. Sinclair (1991) points out that in corpus-based studies, although any co-occurrence of two or more words within a short distance may be a collocation, a frequency of 3 is a statistically significant criterion for judging collocation

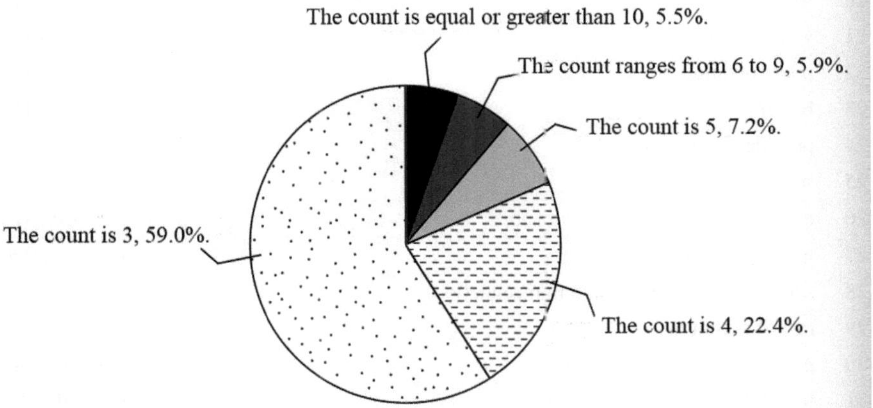

Fig. 3.7 Frequency ratio of automatically extracted candidate chunks

Table 3.3 Reverse MI score list of automatically extracted candidate chunks (partial)

No.	Candidate chunks	Freq.	MI score
1	mutually beneficial	3	7.024 871 426
2	sincere apologies	3	6.801 727 874
3	warning marks	3	6.619 406 318
4	relative documents will be mailed	3	6.331 724 245
5	ocean transportation	3	6.290 902 251
6	completely different articles	3	6.267 645 388
7	carried in one container	3	6.225 114 51
8	settle the problem	3	6.197 449 082
9	transaction prove to be successful	3	6.147 801 407
10	damaged during transit	4	6.108 580 694
11	right goods to be dispatched	3	5.985 257 478
12	mutual benefit	3	5.954 430 014
13	name and address	5	5.922 642 497
14	clean bill of lading	4	5.834 451 588
15	keep dry	4	5.772 108 457
16	dress materials supplied	4	5.752 815 254
17	too inferior to be suitable for the requirements	4	5.661 004 1
18	representative selection	4	5.520 794 029
19	small profit	3	5.520 794 029
20	working relationship	3	5.502 444 89
21	various types	3	5.484 426 385
22	poor condition	4	5.466 726 808
23	bill of lading	12	5.455 707 412
24	provide a guarantor	3	5.454 654 226
25	selling season	4	5.320 123 333
26	enclosing a copy of our catalogue	3	5.277 102 372
27	meet with your approval	3	5.262 034 996
28	suggest you set out a claim immediately	4	5.257 290 812
29	rate of premium	3	5.255 279 637
30	packed in international standard	3	5.210 094 587
31	found that the quality was not satisfactory	4	5.178 010 38
32	formal agreement	6	5.127 751 441
33	valid until	6	5.127 751 441
34	growing demand	3	5.115 328 921
35	draw your attention	3	5.054 890 093
36	opened in your favor	3	5.050 004 945
37	debit note	4	5.009 968 405

(continued)

Table 3.3 (continued)

No.	Candidate chunks	Freq.	MI score
38	due to sail	3	5.005 734 955
39	both surprised and disappointed	3	4.986 221 598
40	comply with your request	5	4.986 151 723
41	sole agency	10	4.983 651 097
42	get in touch	3	4.968 216 61
43	allow you a discount	3	4.910 999 581
44	bill of exchange	3	4.908 461 459
45	claim to be lodged	4	4.899 924 994
46	have received your letter of april	4	4.876 050 489
47	usual practice	5	4.850 119 704
48	quotation sheet	3	4.764 845 947
49	due to arrive	4	4.730 714 608
50	such being the case	3	4.725 713 25
51	against all risks	5	4.718 721 266
52	illustrated catalogues	3	4.713 987 53
53	unpacking the cases	4	4.683 515 22
54	entirely satisfactory	4	4.661 661 711
55	under separate cover	4	4.588 826 757
56	under the captioned contract	4	4.552 475 505
57	end of this month	11	4.467 557 335
58	reach you in good time	4	4.383 394 064
59	irrevocable letter of credit	13	4.365 823 83
60	good condition when they left here	4	4.313 018 939
61	sole agents	3	4.305 771 388
62	requirements of this market	4	4.295 118 033
63	do not hesitate to let us know	3	4.294 128 207
64	look forward to receiving your further orders	3	4.274 283 807
65	local conditions	3	4.268 031 06
66	shipping advice	8	4.200 891 758
67	look forward to your early settlement	4	4.172 781 589
68	payment of the balance	3	4.165 019 017
69	must stress	4	4.162 670 545
70	make clear beforehand	3	4.101 840 984
71	make this request	5	4.035 092 668
72	special care	3	4.029 139 152
73	usual terms of payment	3	3.996 869 119
74	hope you will reconsider	3	3.976 978 696

(continued)

Table 3.3 (continued)

No.	Candidate chunks	Freq.	MI score
75	thank you in advance for your cooperation	4	3.959 100 562
76	hope our explanation will be satisfactory	4	3.958 126 625
77	large quantities	6	3.939 526 993
78	look forward to your early reply	13	3.877 616 216
79	defer payment	3	3.857 288 895
80	which the port of destination and our order number	3	3.848 086 036
81	other suppliers	5	3.846 817 595
82	interested in our proposal	3	3.845 912 208
83	sent herewith	4	3.844 216 814
84	sales promotion	3	3.789 466 299
85	want to know	5	3.786 192 973
86	prepared to consider	3	3.773 741 527
87	good reputation	3	3.741 457 08
88	sales confirmation	16	3.705 584 815
89	above address	7	3.692 666 915
90	reduction in your price	3	3.673 477 337
91	supply from stock	3	3.669 738 042
92	serve you well	3	3.648 244 852
93	feel confident	3	3.623 674 044
94	counter offer	7	3.611 839 586
95	cash discount	4	3.594 924 631
96	latest catalogue	4	3.594 924 631
97	kindly requested	3	3.569 606 823
98	an early reply will be obliged	3	3.561 825 978
99	an exceptional case	3	3.558 146 656
100	enclosed herewith	3	3.556 534 741
101	prompt attention	5	3.552 904 973
102	look forward to the pleasure of your orders	3	3.547 081 743
103	not up to the standard of samples	4	3.545 467 588
104	only reason	3	3.543 631 336
105	partial shipment	5	3.519 314 029
106	date of invoice	3	3.510 810 88
107	drawn up	4	3.505 891 008
108	price lists	3	3.498 510 901
109	regret to tell you	3	3.494 329 27
110	sign and return one copy for our file	3	3.489 739 732
111	thank you for your inquiry	4	3.480 222 252

(continued)

Table 3.3 (continued)

No.	Candidate chunks	Freq.	MI score
112	quantity discount	3	3.479 092 815
113	lower than	4	3.467 739 242
114	reply at your earliest convenience	3	3.446 773 873
115	shipment to be made	4	3.421 755 262
116	pleased to enclose our order no.	3	3.403 940 556
117	packed in cartons	4	3.392 335 602
118	favorable reply	6	3.389 480 656
119	well aware	3	3.389 480 656
120	terms of payment	16	3.381 795 722
121	goods in question were carefully packed by experienced workmen	4	3.331 674 383
122	shipping documents	10	3.325 423 02
123	per dozen	11	3.321 327 298
124	pleased to inform	14	3.291 078 855
125	present salary	3	3.283 241 406
126	claim form	3	3.255 949 264
127	so that we can	6	3.240 720 843
128	good prospects	5	3.240 681 792
129	above mentioned	5	3.222 663 286
130	good enough	6	3.181 841 292
131	dear sir or madam	6	3.180 971 417
132	at the same time	8	3.157 630 525
133	time of shipment	5	3.151 023 247
134	early decision	3	3.146 749 972
135	special discount	4	3.138 166 228
136	under the policy	3	3.136 458 286
137	quite satisfactory	4	3.135 605 407
138	date of delivery	3	3.117 493 262
139	by draft at sight	5	3.110 941 52
140	more than	7	3.099 368 259
141	ready for shipment	4	3.070 726 512
142	please let me know	4	3.061 352 339
143	at an early date	9	3.025 391 806
144	thank you for your letter	43	3.022 798 161
145	satisfied with the quality	3	3.006 184 763

A. Two-word chunk list

From the candidate chunks with $N = 2$ (see Table 3.4), it is found that proper names and commodity-specific names are not included in chunks, such as "New York, San Francisco, Hong Kong, paper bags, iron nails, cotton sweaters, office manager, laser printer, silk blouses, electronic products, plastic furniture, window frames, frying pan, swimming trousers", to name just a few. Abbreviations like "CFR (Cost and Freight) basis" are also not considered as chunks. The following candidate chunks are polysemic, referring to the coexistence of many possible meanings for a word or phrase,[4] and not pertain to chunks. For example, "poor condition" has multiple meanings: (1) bad condition; (2) poor quality. "Sole agents": (1) general agents; (2) exclusive agents; (3) underwriters. "Sole agency": (1) exclusive selling agency; (2) sole agents. "Sales promotion: (1) motivating buying behavior; (2) sales; (3) a marketing strategy; (4) the activity or business of selling products or services market, "Debit note": (1) a debit list; (2) a debit notice; (3) a collection note. "Claim form": (1) a claim form (an application form); (2) a reminder; (3) a form to use when filing a claim. "Less than": (1) less than (in terms of quantity); (2) smaller than; (3) under certain standard; (4) insufficient. "Usual practice": (1) conventions; (2) routines; (3) usual approaches. "Good prospects": (1) hopes; (2) a good future. "Drawn up": (1) drafting, (2) stopping; (3) making something close. "Selling season": (1) the periods during which commodities are sold; (2) peak season. "More than": (1) more than (in terms of quantity); (2) beyond; (3) more than (in comparison to somebody or something). "Special care": (1) special nursing care; (2) carefulness. Among the candidate chunks with $N = 2$, there are 14 proper names and product-specific names, 1 abbreviation, and 13 polysemous chunks. The rest 53 chunks were included in the business English letter chunks for MT.

B. Three-word chunk list

From chunks with $N = 3$ (see Table 3.5), "Bank of China" and "light industrial products" are proper nouns, and "CIF (Cost Insurance and Freight) New York" and "in an FCL (Full Container Load) container" contain abbreviations, which are not included in chunks. The following polysemous candidates are also excluded. "Bill of exchange" has multiple meanings: (1) a draft or money order; (2) deposit of money; (3) bank collection. "Bill of lading": (1) a delivery order; (2) a document containing full particulars of goods shipped or for shipment; (3) a waybill. "Terms and conditions": (1) clauses; (2) contract terms; (3) rate schedule. "In due course": (1) at the right moment; (2) in time; (3) in natural order. "Date of delivery": (1) delivery period; (2) shipping date; (3) date of trade. Among the candidate chunks with $N = 3$, 2 of them are proper nouns and product-specific names, 2 are abbreviations, and 5 belong to polysemy. Therefore, the remaining 47 chunks are taken into consideration.

[4] Polysemy analysis are based on *Oxford Dictionary of Business English for Learners of English* (2011 edition), *Oxford Advanced Learner's English-Chinese Dictionary* (7th edition), *Collins COBUILD Advanced Learners' English-Chinese Dictionary* (2011 Edition), *The English-Chinese Dictionary* (2007 2nd edition), *The 21st Century Unabridged English-Chinese Dictionary* (2005 edition) and so on.

Table 3.4 Automatically extracted candidate chunks ($N = 2$)

No.	Candidate chunks	No.	Candidate chunks
1	working relationship	11	sole agents
2	present salary	12	good enough
3	only reason	13	entirely satisfactory
4	representative selection	14	small profit
5	poor condition	15	special discount
6	office manager	16	feel confident
7	early decision	17	sole agency
8	local conditions	18	sales promotion
9	defer payment	19	sent herewith
10	cash discount	20	shipping documents
21	sincere apologies	52	other suppliers
22	kindly requested	53	quotation sheet
23	enclosed herewith	54	illustrated catalogues
24	price lists	55	cfr basis
25	various types	56	special care
26	iron nails	57	latest catalogue
27	last year	58	per dozen
28	last week	59	drawn up
29	above mentioned	60	sales confirmation
30	san francisco	61	prompt attention
31	mutually beneficial	62	selling season
32	shipping advice	63	hong kong
33	debit note	64	partial shipment
34	cotton sweaters	65	valid until
35	per hundred	66	silk blouses
36	must stress	67	brisk demand
37	quantity discount	68	good reputation
38	claim form	69	large quantities
39	lower than	70	electronic products
40	mutual benefit	71	plastic furniture
41	regular customers	72	window frames
42	keep dry	73	more than
43	paper bags	74	above address
44	warning marks	75	frying pan
45	ocean transportation	76	new york
46	laser printer	77	Counter offer
47	favorable reply	78	growing demand
48	less than	79	swimming trousers

(continued)

Table 3.4 (continued)

No.	Candidate chunks	No.	Candidate chunks
49	usual practice	80	formal agreement
50	good prospects	81	quite satisfactory
51	well aware	–	–

Table 3.5 Automatically extracted candidate chunks ($N = 3$)

No.	Candidate chunks	No.	Candidate chunks
1	serve you well	15	damaged during transit
2	past four years	16	unpacking the cases
3	make clear beforehand	17	prepared to consider
4	goods are shipped	18	completely different articles
5	no available space	19	dress materials supplied
6	in full settlement	20	after careful examination
7	pleased to inform	21	settle the problem
8	date of invoice	22	draw your attention
9	prices we quoted	23	two years ago
10	having carefully considered	24	enter into business
11	an exceptional case	25	bank of china
12	provide a guarantor	26	due to sail
13	due to arrive	27	under separate cover
14	a thousand tons	28	in wooden cases
29	packed in cartons	43	want to know
30	avoid subsequent amendments	44	against all risks
31	time of shipment	45	rate of premium
32	date of delivery	46	under the policy
33	may rest assured	47	terms and conditions
34	in due course	48	get in touch
35	not later than	49	upon receipt of
36	terms of payment	50	most favorable price
37	maintain friendly relations	51	within two months
38	ready for shipment	52	cif new york
39	very brisk demands	53	bill of exchange
40	light industrial products	54	make this request
41	name and address	55	bill of lading
42	supply from stock	56	with keen interest

C. Four-word chunk list

As for the candidate chunks with $N = 4$ (see Table 3.6), "Commercial Bank of Shanghai" is a proper noun. "Such being the case" has multiple meanings: (1) the fact that it is so; (2) in this case. "In the near future": (1) soon; (2) in the near term; (3) the day is in sight. "At the same time": (1) meanwhile; (2) however. "As soon as possible": (1) as early as possible; (2) with the least delay possible. The above 4 candidates are also not listed as chunks. Therefore, the remaining 47 chunks are valid.

Table 3.6 Automatically extracted candidate chunks ($N = 4$)

No.	Candidate chunks	No.	Candidate chunks
1	dear sir or madam	3	at an early date
2	allow you a discount	4	a wide range of
5	be glad to learn	29	hope you will reconsider
6	packed in international standard	30	such being the case
7	regret to tell you	31	push the sales of
8	payment of the balance	32	in an fcl container
9	commercial bank of shanghai	33	usual terms of payment
10	apply for an overdraft	34	by draft at sight
11	both surprised and disappointed	35	so that we can
12	find a ready sale	36	satisfied with the quality
13	interested in our proposal	37	in the near future
14	saving in freight charges	38	within the next month
15	regret to note that	39	opened in your favor
16	clean bill of lading	40	irrevocable letter of credit
17	your claim on order	41	have not yet received
18	claim to be lodged	42	do your utmost to
19	requirements of this market	43	under the captioned contract
20	regret to inform you	44	additional saving on insurance
21	comply with your request	45	carried in one container
22	duly received the documents	46	on a cash basis
23	please let me know	47	settle their account directly
24	reduction in your price	48	am writing to ask
25	within the contracted time	49	at the same time
26	end of this month	50	shipment to be made
27	meet with your approval	51	on the other hand
28	from date of invoice	52	as soon as possible

D. Five-word chunk list

When N = 5 (see Table 3.7), "Commercial Bank of Hong Kong" is a proper noun and product-specific name. The remaining 29 chunks are seen as chunks in this research.

E. Six-word chunk list

Among the chunks with $N = 6$ (see Table 3.8), "National City Bank of New York" and "The People's Insurance Company of China" are excluded because they are proper nouns, so the rest 29 chunks are taken as valid chunks.

F. Seven-word chunk list

Since there are fewer candidate chunks with $N = 7$, 8 and 9, they are analyzed together (see Tables 3.9, 3.10 and 3.11). It is found that all 40 chunks conform to meet the criteria of business English letter chunks in MT.

G. Extraction results of chunks with two to nine words

In this chapter, there are 45 invalid chunks (accounting for about 16%). And the remaining 245 chunks are organized into a table of business English letter chunks, as shown in Table 3.12.

Table 3.7 Automatically extracted candidate chunks ($N = 5$)

No.	Candidate chunks	No.	Candidate chunks
1	contract to be drawn up	16	one of the leading importers
2	a sole agency for marketing	17	place regular and substantial orders
3	many thanks for your quotation	18	have quoted such low prices
4	reach you in good time	19	to place a trial order
5	commercial bank of hong kong	20	thank you for your inquiry
6	on going into the matter	21	order number should be stenciled
7	right goods to be dispatched	22	please see to it that
8	dispatched to you at once	23	date and place of expiry
9	relative documents will be mailed	24	in reply to your letter
10	the shipping containers we provide	25	full set of shipping documents
11	through a confusion of number	26	can be loaded and locked
12	many thanks for your letter	27	a full range of samples
13	transaction prove to be successful	28	reply at your earliest convenience
14	the delivery date is approaching	29	thank you for your letter
15	the said license is approved	30	cancel part of the order

Table 3.8 Automatically extracted candidate chunks ($N = 6$)

No.	Candidate chunks	No.	Candidate chunks
1	lead to further business between us	4	an early reply will be obliged
2	pleased to enclose our order no	5	prompt reply will be greatly appreciated
3	quite willing to undertake the training	6	until the end of this year
7	a trial period of twelve months	20	the people's insurance company of china
8	these prices include packing and delivery	21	look forward to your early reply
9	sorry to learn from your letter	22	hope you will reconsider this matter
10	a fair comparison of quality	23	be packed in international standard tea
11	hope our explanation will be satisfactory	24	hope to hear favorably from you
12	have received your letter of april	25	national city bank of new york
13	good condition when they left here	26	early reply will be highly appreciated
14	must return the goods to you	27	enclosing a copy of our catalogue
15	look forward to your early settlement	28	can be opened at both ends
16	above will be acceptable to you	29	find both quality and prices satisfactory
17	in urgent need of these goods	30	by the end of this month
18	make delivery at an early date	31	at the end of each month
19	in this particular line of business	–	–

Table 3.9 Automatically extracted candidate chunks ($N = 7$)

No.	Candidate chunks
1	defer payment for a further three weeks
2	look forward to receiving your further orders
3	load and unload at the same time
4	suggest you set out a claim immediately
5	a claim immediately against the shipping company
6	found that the quality was not satisfactory
7	not up to the standard of samples
8	have no choice but to do so
9	did not contain the goods you ordered
10	our offer remains valid for one month
11	accept your quotation would mean little profit
12	do not hesitate to let us know
13	thank you in advance for your cooperation
14	shipping space has been fully booked up

Table 3.10 Automatically extracted candidate chunks ($N = 8$)

No.	Candidate chunks
1	certainly do our best to make it so
2	be willing to establish business relations with us
3	welcome the opportunity to do business with you
4	forced to cut our prices to the minimum
5	convince you of the reasonableness of our quotation
6	for the invoice value and inspection charges involved
7	too inferior to be suitable for the requirements
8	a mistake is indeed made in the packing
9	please send us your proforma invoice in triplicate
10	place more substantial orders on a regular basis
11	on the outer packing please mark our initials
12	look forward to the pleasure of your order
13	payment by confirmed and irrevocable letter of credit
14	the wide range of goods we deal in
15	be aware of the wide range of goods
16	sign and return one copy for our file

Table 3.11 Automatically extracted candidate chunks ($N = 9$)

No.	Candidate chunks
1	which the port of destination and our order number
2	a ready sale for our products in your market
3	goods in question were carefully packed by experienced workmen
4	the survey report issued by beijing commodity inspection bureau
5	the goods delivered is not up to the standard
6	many years experience in this particular line of business
7	indeed sorry that you found our price too high
8	all the terms contained in the offer are acceptable
9	contained in the offer are acceptable except the price
10	early as possible by direct steamer to hong kong

3.5 Summary

This chapter provides key technologies for an MT-oriented corresponding chunk bank in business correspondences from English to Chinese. Through the three modules of "text pre-processing, automatic extraction and manual processing", the human–computer interaction in business English corresponding chunk extraction based on

Table 3.12 MT-oriented business English letter chunk list

No.	Original serial number	Candidate chunks	*N* gram
1	4798	working relationship	2
2	9986	present salary	2
3	10007	only reason	2
4	16721	representative selection	2
5	22537	early decision	2
6	22689	local conditions	2
7	27160	defer payment	2
8	28885	cash discount	2
9	32170	good enough	2
10	38557	entirely satisfactory	2
11	41881	small profit	2
12	42463	special discount	2
13	44317	feel confident	2
14	57451	sent herewith	2
15	58930	shipping documents	2
16	62195	sincere apologies	2
17	63651	kindly requested	2
18	68030	enclosed herewith	2
19	68762	price lists	2
20	68799	various types	2
21	69685	last year	2
22	71210	last week	2
23	74449	above mentioned	2
24	81040	mutually beneficial	2
25	83754	shipping advice	2
26	89250	per hundred	2
27	91051	must stress	2
28	91311	quantity discount	2
29	93385	lower than	2
30	96467	mutual benefit	2
31	59930	regular customers	2
32	97377	keep dry	2
33	98959	warning marks	2
34	99610	ocean transportation	2
35	105009	favorable reply	2
36	111579	well aware	2

(continued)

Table 3.12 (continued)

No.	Original serial number	Candidate chunks	*N* gram
37	113157	other suppliers	2
38	113189	quotation sheet	2
39	113720	illustrated catalogues	2
40	115471	latest catalogue	2
41	116751	per dozen	2
42	117474	sales confirmation	2
43	121457	prompt attention	2
44	125354	partial shipment	2
45	126626	valid until	2
46	128580	brisk demand	2
47	130655	good reputation	2
48	131380	large quantities	2
49	140569	above address	2
50	144234	counter offer	2
51	144249	growing demand	2
52	152019	formal agreement	2
53	152929	quite satisfactory	2
54	13310	serve you well	3
55	14440	past four years	3
56	20567	make clear beforehand	3
57	23504	goods are shipped	3
58	23687	no available space	3
59	28936	in full settlement	3
60	29315	pleased to inform	3
61	40791	date of invoice	3
62	42553	prices we quoted	3
63	43795	having carefully considered	3
64	45260	an exceptional case	3
65	46811	provide a guarantor	3
66	53728	due to arrive	3
67	56358	a thousand tons	3
68	57490	damaged during transit	3
69	58084	unpacking the cases	3
70	58427	prepared to consider	3
71	58999	completely different articles	3
72	61364	dress materials supplied	3

(continued)

Table 3.12 (continued)

No.	Original serial number	Candidate chunks	*N* gram
73	61400	after careful examination	3
74	64061	settle the problem	3
75	68443	draw your attention	3
76	77261	two years ago	3
77	80714	enter into business	3
78	83798	due to sail	3
79	88878	under separate cover	3
80	88933	with keen interest	3
81	95401	in wooden cases	3
82	95582	packed in cartons	3
83	101893	avoid subsequent amendment	3
84	102522	time of shipment	3
85	114413	may rest assured	3
86	115058	not later than	3
87	115450	terms of payment	3
88	116774	maintain friendly relations	3
89	120629	ready for shipment	3
90	128645	very brisk demands	3
91	130634	name and address	3
92	132113	supply from stock	3
93	135671	want to know	3
94	137956	against all risks	3
95	138991	rate of premium	3
96	139130	under the policy	3
97	142813	get in touch	3
98	144216	upon receipt of	3
99	144223	most favorable price	3
100	144230	within two months	3
101	149386	make this request	3
102	3827	dear sir or madam	4
103	4301	allow you a discount	4
104	17093	at an early date	4
105	17510	a wide range of	4
106	17529	be glad to learn	4
107	20775	packed in international standard	4
108	23485	regret to tell you	4

(continued)

Table 3.12 (continued)

No.	Original serial number	Candidate chunks	*N* gram
109	30780	payment of the balance	4
110	35160	apply for an overdraft	4
111	36586	both surprised and disappointed	4
112	44950	find a ready sale	4
113	46104	interested in our proposal	4
114	55092	saving in freight charges	4
115	57584	regret to note that	4
116	57601	clean bill of lading	4
117	57604	your claim on order	4
118	57658	claim to be lodged	4
119	58094	requirements of this market	4
120	58254	regret to inform you	4
121	60086	comply with your request	4
122	61511	duly received the documents	4
123	66000	please let me know	4
124	67951	reduction in your price	4
125	73731	within the contracted time	4
126	83853	end of this month	4
127	84635	meet with your approval	4
128	89293	from date of invoice	4
129	90653	hope you will reconsider	4
130	101893	avoid subsequent amendments	4
131	102608	usual terms of payment	4
132	102695	by draft at sight	4
133	104190	so that we can	4
134	115480	satisfied with the quality	4
135	115506	within the next month	4
136	118138	opened in your favor	4
137	120779	irrevocable letter of credit	4
138	122024	have not yet received	4
139	123306	do your utmost to	4
140	123314	under the captioned contract	4
141	124398	additional saving on insurance	4
142	124415	carried in one container	4
143	127043	on a cash basis	4
144	132235	settle their account directly	4

(continued)

Table 3.12 (continued)

No.	Original serial number	Candidate chunks	*N* gram
145	139132	am writing to ask	4
146	144309	shipment to be made	4
147	151624	on the other hand	4
148	5123	contract to be drawn up	4
149	10893	a sole agency for marketing	5
150	17522	many thanks for your quotation	5
151	21662	reach you in good time	5
152	47560	on going into the matter	5
153	47600	right goods to be dispatched	5
154	47611	dispatched to you at once	5
155	47614	relative documents will be mailed	5
156	55248	the shipping containers we provide	5
157	61052	through a confusion of number	5
158	65279	many thanks for your letter	5
159	71950	transaction prove to be successful	5
160	74102	the delivery date is approaching	5
161	77426	the said license is approved	5
162	80835	one of the leading importers	5
163	90147	place regular and substantial orders	5
164	90177	have quoted such low prices	5
165	90610	to place a trial order	5
166	91356	thank you for your inquiry	5
167	97450	order number should be stenciled	5
168	101838	please see to it that	5
169	103797	date and place of expiry	5
170	122926	in reply to your letter	5
171	123681	full set of shipping documents	5
172	126122	can be loaded and locked	5
173	132443	a full range of samples	5
174	135741	reply at your earliest convenience	5
175	140133	thank you for your letter	5
176	149882	cancel part of the order	5
177	2529	lead to further business between us	5
178	6003	pleased to enclose our order no.	6
179	8287	quite willing to undertake the training	6
180	24065	an early reply will be obliged	6

(continued)

Table 3.12 (continued)

No.	Original serial number	Candidate chunks	*N* gram
181	24782	prompt reply will be greatly appreciated	6
182	33751	until the end of this year	6
183	37516	a trial period of twelve months	6
184	40917	these prices include packing and delivery	6
185	42649	sorry to learn from your letter	6
186	45512	a fair comparison of quality	6
187	57722	hope our explanation will be satisfactory	6
188	57754	have received your letter of april	6
189	57781	good condition when they left here	6
190	58194	must return the goods to you	6
191	58199	look forward to your early settlement	6
192	68930	above will be acceptable to you	6
193	72467	in urgent need of these goods	6
194	72496	make delivery at an early date	6
195	78045	in this particular line of business	6
196	88255	look forward to your early reply	6
197	90771	hope you will reconsider this matter	6
198	99196	be packed in international standard tea	6
199	102340	hope to hear favorably from you	6
200	104709	early reply will be highly appreciated	6
201	117328	enclosing a copy of our catalogue	6
202	125311	can be opened at both ends	6
203	146079	find both quality and prices satisfactory	6
204	146700	by the end of this month	6
205	151675	at the end of each month	6
206	27018	defer payment for a further three weeks	6
207	48722	look forward to receiving your further orders	7
208	55417	load and unload at the same time	7
209	57716	suggest you set out a claim immediately	7
210	57732	a claim immediately against the shipping company	7
211	58232	found that the quality was not satisfactory	7
212	58296	not up to the standard of samples	7
213	60262	have no choice but to do so	7
214	61193	did not contain the goods you ordered	7
215	88805	our offer remains valid for one month	7
216	90695	accept your quotation would mean little profit	7

(continued)

Table 3.12 (continued)

No.	Original serial number	Candidate chunks	*N* gram
217	96055	do not hesitate to let us know	7
218	100362	thank you in advance for your cooperation	7
219	124873	shipping space has been fully booked up	7
220	2582	certainly do our best to make it so	8
221	25398	be willing to establish business relations with us	8
222	42198	welcome the opportunity to do business with you	8
223	43711	forced to cut our prices to the minimum	8
224	45418	convince you of the reasonableness of our quotation	8
225	58246	for the invoice value and inspection charges involved	8
226	58328	too inferior to be suitable for the requirements	8
227	61227	a mistake is indeed made in the packing	8
228	73625	please send us your proforma invoice in triplicate	8
229	90835	place more substantial orders on a regular basis	8
230	99455	on the outer packing please mark our initials	8
231	102894	look forward to the pleasure of your order	8
232	107015	payment by confirmed and irrevocable letter of credit	8
233	117310	the wide range of goods we deal in	8
234	117358	be aware of the wide range of goods	8
235	121561	sign and return one copy for our file	8
236	21108	which the port of destination and our order number	9
237	45163	a ready sale for our products in your market	9
238	57893	goods in question were carefully packed by experienced workmen	9
239	58258	the survey report issued by beijing commodity inspection bureau	9
240	58298	the goods delivered is not up to the standard	9
241	81998	many years experience in this particular line of business	9
242	90087	indeed sorry that you found our price too high	9
243	90756	all the terms contained in the offer are acceptable	9
244	90769	contained in the offer are acceptable except the price	9
245	114797	early as possible by direct steamer to hong kong	9

parallel corpus is realized. First, 400 business letters in English and the corresponding Chinese versions (115,026 words in total, accounting for about one-tenth of the total corpus, including 46,868 words in English and 68,158 in Chinese) were randomly extracted from the English-Chinese parallel corpus with a total of about 1 million words, with text preprocessed. With the help of the chunk extraction system, 202,127 g in business English letters were automatically extracted according to 2–9 g.

and 154,613 g were obtained after automatic de-emphasis processing. Among them, the Grams with a frequency higher than 2 were calculated through the MI method, and 290 chunks were obtained in business English letters. After manual processing, 245 MT-oriented business English letter chunks are obtained eventually. In Chap. 4, we will probe into the MT-oriented chunks in business English correspondences, identify the translations and explore their corresponding relationship by analysis of examples, and develop corresponding rules and standard scores.

References

Feng, Y., & Wang, L. (1999). A quantitative study of collocational of words in English. *Foreign Language Teaching Abroad, 2*, 5–10.

Sinclair, J. M. (1991). *Corpus, concordance, collocation.* Oxford University Press.

Wang, L. (2006). Quantitative analysis method of collocational patterns. *Journal of Shanghai Normal University (Philosophy & Social Sciences Edition), 6*, 117–122.

Wei, N. X., & Li, J. J. (2013). A new computing method for extracting contiguous phraseological sequences from academic text corpora. *International Journal of Corpus Linguistics, 18*(4), 506–535.

Zhan, H. (2011). Tools and methods for extracting chunks from corpus. *Foreign Language Teaching, 2*, 23–26.

Chapter 4
Corresponding Relationship and Rules

4.1 Introduction

On the basis of the table of MT-oriented business English letter chunks shown in Chap. 3, this chapter will study the corresponding relationship and rules between chunks and Chinese translations. With the help of the retrieval function of ParaConc, the MT-oriented business English letter chunks and corresponding example sentences are searched and further analyzed in order to summarize their corresponding relationship and rules, set down corresponding rules and standard scores, and develop the table of the MT-oriented corresponding chunks in English-Chinese business letters.

4.2 Corresponding Chunk Retrieval Tools and Methods

Since translating highly depends on context, the translator interacts with text, readers and others. Good translations will be accepted and repeated while bad ones be rejected and discarded. Recurrence of translation equivalents embodies the consensus of community interaction, and the crystallization of collective wisdom (Teubert, 2002). Therefore, through the retrieval function provided by the ParaConc (Fig. 4.1) on the basis of the self-built corpus (400 business English letters and corresponding Chinese translations randomly selected from the parallel corpus mentioned in Chap. 3, which has been processed into sentence alignment, a total of 115,026 words), we retrieve the MT-oriented chunks in business English correspondences, determine the corresponding translations and discuss the corresponding relationship through sentence analysis, and formulate corresponding rules and standard scores.

F. Hu, *An MT-Oriented Study of Corresponding Lexical Chunks in Business Correspondences from English to Chinese*,
https://doi.org/10.1007/978-981-99-4977-9_4

Fig. 4.1 ParaConc interface

4.3 Classification of Corresponding Relationship and Rules

Through analysis, it is found that there is no complete one-to-one correspondence between MT-oriented corresponding chunks and translations in English-Chinese business correspondences, which verifies the view that "the translation phenomenon of the same original text corresponding to various translations as well as the phenomenon of synonymy in linguistics" proposed by Lu and Wei (2012). Their relationships are classified into three types: complete correspondence, incomplete correspondence, and zero correspondence (indicating that there is no translation).

Based on the classification, relevant corresponding rules and representation methods are developed as follows:

First, there are three symbols: "=" for complete correspondence, "≈" for incomplete correspondence, and "*" for zero correspondence.

Second, "E" stands for the MT-oriented chunks in business English letters while "C" for the corresponding Chinese translations.

Third, the original serial number is a unique code automatically assigned by the chunk extraction system in order to find the original sentence in the text if necessary.

Fourth, in the incomplete correspondence, "a, b, c, …" indicates different Chinese translations of the same original text.

Fifth, the corresponding ratio is expressed in percent (1–100%), which is converted to the standard score with a range between 1 and 100. Based on the score, priority correspondence matching of MT-oriented chunks in business English correspondences and their corresponding Chinese translations will be performed accordingly.

The following examples are used as samples to illustrate the types of correspondence and the related corresponding rules and representations.

The sentences containing the English chunk (in bold) with the original serial number 44950 are as follows.

Table 4.1 Corresponding rule and standard score of chunks with original serial number 44950

Original serial number	Chunk	Chinese translation	Corresponding rule	Standard score
44950	E44950 = find a ready sale	C44950 = 畅销	E44950 = C44950	100

(1) We are confident that you will **find a ready sale** for our products in your market. (我们相信这些产品在你方市场上很畅销。)
(2) These silk garments **find a ready sale** in the UK. (这些丝绸衣物在英国市场很畅销。)
(3) We are sure you will **find a ready sale** for our products in New York and we do hope we can reach an agreement. (我们肯定你方将会发现我公司产品在纽约十分畅销。同时我们期待双方能达成一致协议。)

In these example sentences, the original serial number of "find a ready sale" is 44950, and its frequency in the corpus is 3. After analysis, it is found that all of the corresponding translations is "畅销". Therefore, they are in complete correspondence and the correspondence rule is E44950 = C44950, where E44950 stands for "find a ready sale" and C44950 for "best seller". The corresponding ratio is 100% and the standard score is 100 (see Table 4.1).

A. Complete correspondence and its corresponding rules

Business letters mainly convey specific information about foreign trade business or stipulate the responsibilities and rights of buyers and sellers, such as price, payment terms, packaging, shipment, insurance claims, etc. The statement must be accurate and precise, otherwise they might cause disputes or claims. Therefore, most of the MT-oriented chunks in English-Chinese business correspondences are in complete correspondence.

For example, some chunks such as "find a ready sale", "enclosed herewith", "within the contracted time", etc., can be easily translated by simply adopting the corresponding chunks. In this sense, the key to detecting the standardization and accuracy of MT lies in the use of corresponding chunks.

In this chapter, 30 MT-oriented chunks in complete correspondence (including 10 two-word chunks, 5 three-word or four-word chunks, and 2 chunks containing five to nine words) in English-Chinese business letters with example sentences in the parallel corpus are randomly selected and illustrated in the following part.

a. Two-word chunks[1]

The sentences containing the chunk with the original serial number 4798 (in bold) are listed as follows:

(1) We have always valued the happy **working relationship** that has existed over so many years between our two firms, and shall do our best to maintain it. (本

[1] There are 10 chunks in total, sorted by the original serial number.

公司非常满意我们之间多年来愉快的工作关系，并竭尽全力维持这种友好关系。)

(2) We hope that our handling of your first order will lead to further business between us and mark the beginning of good **working relationship**. (希望对贵方第一个订单的处理将带来双方进一步的合作，并成为双方良好工作关系开始的标志。)

(3) As you may not be aware of the wide range of goods we deal in, we are enclosing a copy of our catalogue and hope that our handing of your first order with us will lead to further business between us and mark the beginning of a happy **working relationship**. (您也许对我方的商品交易范围不太了解，现随函附上一份产品目录，希望自此订单开始，彼此建立更多的业务来往，展开愉快的工作关系。)

In these example sentences, the original serial number of "working relationship" is 4798 with a frequency of 3. It shows that the corresponding Chinese translations are all "工作关系". Therefore, they are in complete correspondence, and the corresponding rule is E4798 = C4798, where E4798 stands for "working relationship" and C4798 for "工作关系". The corresponding ratio is 100%, and the standard score is 100 (see Table 4.2).

The sentences containing the chunk with the original serial number 16721 (in bold) are listed as follows:

(1) We therefore suggest that we first test the market by sending you a **representative selection** of our products, for sale on our account. (因此，我公司建议，我们寄送具有代表性的产品，由贵公司代为销售，一试市场状况。)

(2) We thank you for your letter of 25th August and accept with pleasure your proposal to send us a **representative selection** of your plastics on a consignment basis. (感谢贵公司 8 月 25 日来信，并乐意接受有关寄售贵公司具有代表性的塑胶制品的提议。)

(3) We have carefully considered your proposal to receive a trial delivery of our frying pan on consignment and are sending you a **representative selection** of our most popular lines. (贵公司建议以寄售方式试销一批我公司生产的平底锅，经我公司仔细考虑后，随即运去一批具有代表性的最畅销货物。)

(4) We have considered your proposal to receive a trial delivery of our cutlery on consignment and are sending you a **representative selection** of our most popular lines. 我方已考虑贵方关于用寄售的方式销售我方刀具的建议，现选出极受欢迎的具有代表性的一批货品发往贵方。

Table 4.2 Corresponding rule and standard score of chunks with original serial number 4798

Original serial number	Chunk	Chinese translation	Corresponding rule	Standard score
4798	E4798 = working relationship	C4798 = 工作关系	E4798 = C4798	100

In these example sentences, the original serial number of "representative selection" is 16721, with a frequency of 4. From the above sentences, it is found that all of them are translated into "具有代表性". Therefore, they are in complete correspondence, and the corresponding rule can be expressed as E16721 = C16721, where E16721 stands for "representative selection" and C16721 for "具有代表性". The corresponding ratio is 100%, and the standard score is 100 (see Table 4.3).

The sentences containing the chunk with the original serial number 32170 (in bold) are listed as follows:

(1) Please be **good enough** to confirm that you accept the appointment on the terms stated and that you will be able to commence your duties on 1st September. (请您**最好**向我们证实接受这个职位及其附带条件, 那么可以在 9 月1 日开始您的工作。)
(2) Please be **good enough** to state, which you prefer so that we can arrange your account accordingly. (请您**最好**讲明使用何种付款方式, 以便本公司更好地处理您的账目。)
(3) It may well be that non-payment is due to an oversight and we now ask you to be **good enough** to send us your check within the next few days. (没有清账可能是一时疏忽所致, 本公司请求贵公司**最好**在数日内寄来支票结算账目。)
(4) In March 2007, you were **good enough** grant me a credit of 80,000 RMB, which was repaid within the agreed period. (2007 年 3 月, 贵行**最好**给予本公司人民币 8 万元的贷款, 在指定期内归还。)
(5) Please be **good enough** to provide Mr. Patrick Liu, the bearer, whose signature is given below, with such funds as he may need, within the limit of U.S. $5,000. (敬请贵行**最好**提供持票人刘帕特立克先生 5000 美元以下的款项, 刘先生的签署如下。)
(6) We should like to feel that there has been some misunderstanding and ask you to be **good enough** to explain why the bill was not honored. (本公司相信其中必有误会存在, 请贵公司**最好**解释原因。)

In these example sentences, the original serial number of "good enough" is 32170, which appears 6 times in the corpus. After observation, the corresponding translations are all "最好". Therefore, they are in complete correspondence. The corresponding rule could be expressed as E32170 = C32170, where E32170 stands for "good enough" and C32170 for "最好". The corresponding ratio is 100% and the standard score is 100 (see Table 4.4).

The sentences containing the chunk with the original serial number 41881 (in bold) are listed as follows:

Table 4.3 Corresponding rule and standard score of chunks with original serial number 16721

Original serial number	Chunk	Chinese translation	Corresponding rule	Standard score
16721	E16721 = representative selection	C16721 = 具有代表性	E16721 = C16721	100

Table 4.4 Corresponding rule and standard score of chunks with original serial number 32170

Original serial number	Chunk	Chinese translation	Corresponding rule	Standard score
32170	E32170 = good enough	C32170 = 最好	E32170 = C32170	100

(1) Your payment leaves an unpaid balance of 5,500 RMB and, as our policy is to work on **small profit** margins, we regret that we cannot grant long-term credit facilities. (结账后尚欠款人民币 5500 元整, 而本公司宗旨是薄利推销, 实在无法给予您长期记账服务, 敬请谅解。)
(2) To accept the prices you quote would leave me with only a **small profit** in my sales since this is an area in which the principal is for articles in the medium price range. (假如接受这个价格, 我只有一些薄利可赚, 因为本地区买家主要是购买中等价格的商品。)
(3) Our quoted price leaves us with only a **small profit** and if it were not for the large orders we receive from a number of our regular customers, we could not have quoted for supplies even at that price. (按照这个定价我们只有一些薄利可赚, 如果不是有一批老客户经常下大宗订单的话, 我公司甚至不能以这个定价供货。)

In the above sentences, the original number of "small profit" is 41881, with a frequency of 3. It is found that the corresponding Chinese translations are all "薄利". Therefore, they are in complete correspondence. The corresponding rule could be written as E41881 = C41881, where E41881 stands for "small profit" and C41881 for "薄利". The corresponding ratio is 100% and the standard score is 100 (see Table 4.5).

The sentences containing the chunk with the original serial number 44317 (in bold) are listed as follows:

(1) We **feel confident** that the quality of material used and the high standard of workmanship will appeal to the most selective buyers. (我们自信所用原材料的质量和高标准的工艺会吸引最挑剔的买主。)
(2) When you have a chance to examine them, we **feel confident** that you will agree that the goods are both excellent in quality and very reasonable in price. (敬请贵方审阅, 我们自信能令贵方满意, 因为我方的货物都品质优秀, 价格合理。)
(3) When the goods reach you, we **feel confident** you will be completely satisfied with them at the prices offered they represent exceptional value. (我公司自信

Table 4.5 Corresponding rule and standard score of chunks with original serial number 41881

Original serial number	Chunk	Chinese translation	Corresponding rule	Standard score
41881	E41881 = small profit	C41881 = 薄利	E41881 = C41881	100

货物到达后，您一定会感到完全满意。事实上，以这个价格，这种货物实在是物有所值。)

In these example sentences, the original serial number of "feel confident" is 44317, with a frequency of 3. It is found that the corresponding Chinese translations are all "自信". Therefore, they are in complete correspondence. The corresponding rule is E44317 = C44317, where E44317 stands for "feel confident" and C44317 for "自信". The corresponding ratio is 100%, and the standard score is 100 (see Table 4.6).

The sentences containing the chunk with the original serial number 59930 (in bold) are listed as follows:

(1) Our quoted price leaves us with only a small profit and if it were not for the large orders we receive from a number of our **regular customers**, we could not have quoted for supplies even at that price. (按照这个定价我们只有很少的利润，如果不是有一批老客户经常下大宗订单的话，我公司甚至不能以这个定价供货。)
(2) Our present difficulty is purely temporary. Before the end of this month payments are due to us from a number of our **regular customers** who are notably prompt payers. (我们目前的困难纯粹是暂时性的，在本月底前我公司客户账目到期缴清，那些老客户都是准时结账者。)
(3) We always dislike refusing justified requests of any kind from **regular customers**, but regret for your case we have no choice but to do so. (我们总是不愿意拒绝老客户任何形式的合理要求，但对贵方的特殊情况表示遗憾，我们毫无选择。)
(4) We are naturally disappointed that there should be any need for this request, but we always like to oblige our **regular customers** even at some inconvenience to ourselves. (我公司自然对这个要求很失望，但我们当然乐意便利老客户，甚至因此给自己带来不便，也在所不惜。)
(5) We always dislike refusing requests of any kind from **regular customers**, but regret that on this occasion we have no choice but to do so. (我公司并不拒绝任何由老客户提出的要求，但此时，我公司除了抱歉之外别无其他选择。)

In these example sentences, the original serial number of "regular customers" is 59930, which appears 5 times in the corpus. The corresponding Chinese translations are all "老客户". Therefore, they are in complete correspondence. So the corresponding rule is E59930 = C59930, where E59930 stands for "regular customers" and C59930 for "老客户". The corresponding ratio is 100% and the standard score is 100 (see Table 4.7).

The sentences containing the chunk with the original serial number 68030 (in bold) are listed as follows:

Table 4.6 Corresponding rule and standard score of chunks with original serial number 44317

Original serial number	Chunk	Chinese translation	Corresponding rule	Standard score
44317	E44317 = feel confident	C44317 = 自信	E44317 = C44317	100

Table 4.7 Corresponding rule and standard score of chunks with original serial number 59930

Original serial number	Chunk	Chinese translation	Corresponding rule	Standard score
59930	E59930 = regular customers	C59930 = 老客户	E59930 = C59930	100

(1) As requested, we **enclosed herewith** our sales confirmation in duplicate. (按照贵方要求, 我们已随函附上一式两份的销售确认书。)
(2) We find both quality and prices satisfactory. **Enclosed herewith**, please find our order No. 363. (我们对产品质量和价格都非常满意。随函附上订单, 请查收 363 号。)
(3) A set of samples is **enclosed herewith**. (随函附上一套样品。)

In these example sentences, the original serial number of "enclosed herewith" is 68030, with a frequency of 3. We find that the Chinese translations are all "随函附上". Therefore, they are in complete correspondence. The corresponding rule is E68030 = C68030, where E68030 stands for "enclosed herewith" and C68030 for "随函附上". The corresponding ratio is 100%, converted to the standard score of 100 (see Table 4.8).

The sentences containing the chunk with the original serial number 68762 (in bold) are listed as follows:

(1) In order to acquaint us with the material and workmanship of your products, we shall appreciate it if you will send us your cata1ogues, samples books and **price lists**. (为了熟悉贵方的产品材料和工艺, 如果贵方向我们提供您的产品目录, 样品书和价目表, 我们将非常感谢。)
(2) We enclose our latest **price lists** covering all the products we handle within the framework of your specialized lines. (随函奉上你方经营范围内的我方经营的产品的最新价目表, 请查收。)
(3) We are interested in obtaining catalogues and **price lists** of your embroidered linen products. In particular, we are interested in table linens of various types, such as tablecloths, napkins, and towels. (我们对贵公司绣花亚麻织品的目录和价目表很感兴趣, 尤其是对各种类型的亚麻织品, 如桌布、餐布和餐巾感兴趣。)

In these example sentences, the original serial number of "price lists" is 68762, and its frequency in the corpus is 3. All of its translations are "价目表". Therefore, they are in complete correspondence. Then the corresponding rule could be expressed

Table 4.8 Corresponding rule and standard score of chunks with original serial number 68030

Original serial number	Chunk	Chinese translation	Corresponding rule	Standard score
68030	E68030 = enclosed herewith	C68030 = 随函附上	E68030 = C68030	100

as E68762 = C68762, where E68762 stands for "price lists" and C68762 for "价目表", The corresponding ratio is 100%, converted to the standard score of 100 (see Table 4.9).

The sentences containing the chunk with the original serial number 125354 (in bold) are listed as follows:

(1) As to **partial shipment**, we also stressed its benefit to both parties because we could ship immediately what we had on hand instead of waiting for the whole lot to be completed. (至于分批装运, 我们也强调对双方的利益, 因为我们可以立即装运我们当时有的, 而不是等待整个地段装运的完成。)
(2) After our careful consideration, we find your requirements are not completely reasonable. Therefore, we only approve partial amendment. **Partial shipment** cannot be allowed. "Transshipment prohibited" can be amended to read "transshipment allowed". (仔细考虑之后, 我们发现贵方要求不完全合理, 因此我们只同意做部分修改, 不允许分批装运, "禁止转运"可以修改为"允许转船"。)
(3) Our usual terms of payment are by confirmed, irrevocable letter of credit for the full amount of the invoice value to be established in our favor, available by draft at sight, reaching us one month ahead of shipment, remaining valid for negotiation in China till the 21st day after the prescribed time of shipment, and allowing transshipment and **partial shipment**. (我们的一贯付款条件是采用保兑的、不可撤销的、金额为发票的全部数额的、以我方为抬头人的即期信用证, 于装运前一个月寄至我们。信用证在中国的议付有效期为规定的装运期后 21 天止, 且准许转船和分批装运。)
(4) On perusal, we find that transshipment and **partial shipment** are not allowed. (按规定, 我们发现转运和分批装运都是不允许的。)
(5) We have received your request for transshipment and **partial shipment** today. (今日我们已经收到贵方对转运和分批装运的建议。)

In these example sentences, the original serial number of "partial shipment" is 125354, which appears 5 times in the corpus. Through analysis, all of its translation is "分批装运". Therefore, they are in complete correspondence. The corresponding rule is E125354 = C125354, where E125354 stands for "partial shipment" and C125354 for "分批装运". The ratio is 100% and the standard score is 100 (see Table 4.10).

The sentences containing the chunk with the original serial number 144249 (in bold) are listed as follows:

Table 4.9 Corresponding rule and standard score of chunks with original serial number 68762

Original serial number	Chunk	Chinese translation	Corresponding rule	Standard score
68762	E68762 = price lists	C68762 = 价目表	E68762 = C68762	100

Table 4.10 Corresponding rule and standard score of chunks with original serial number 125354

Original serial number	Chunk	Chinese translation	Corresponding rule	Standard score
125354	E125354 = partial shipment	C125354 = 分批装运	E125354 = C125354	100

Table 4.11 Corresponding rule and standard score of chunks with original serial number 144249

Original serial number	Chunk	Chinese translation	Corresponding rule	Standard score
144249	E144249 = growing demand	C144249 = 不断增长的需求	E144249 = C144249	100

(1) As you are aware that there has been lately a brisk demand for the above commodities, such **growing demand** has doubtlessly resulted in increased prices.
(如你所知, 最近市场对以上产品需求旺盛, 不断增长的需求已毫无疑问引起价格的上涨。)

(2) You would be delighted to know that there is a **growing demand** for the Electric Fans in this market and we should like to place large orders with you if your prices are acceptable.
(想必贵公司已欣悉电风扇在该市场中不断增长的需求，如果贵方的价格可以接受我方将下大的订单。)

(3) It is true that there has recently been a **growing demand** for your class of product, but I doubt whether your expectations of future demand will be fulfilled.
(事实上，最近这里已经对贵公司产品出现不断增长的需求。但我怀疑，您对将来需求的期望能否成为事实。)

In these example sentences, with an original serial number of 144249, "growing demand" appears 3 times in the corpus, and all of them are translated into "不断增长的需求". Therefore, they are in complete correspondence. The corresponding rule is E144249 = C144249, where E144249 stands for "growing demand" and C144249 for "不断增长的需求". The corresponding ratio is 100% and the standard score is 100 (see Table 4.11).

b. Three-word chunks[2]

The sentences containing the chunk with the original serial number 88878 (in bold) are listed as follows:

(1) We are enclosing our illustrated catalogue giving the details you ask for and also **under separate cover** sending you a full range of samples.
(我们随函寄去带有插图的目录, 其中有你们想要的详细资料, 在另函中还邮寄去各式样品。)

[2] There are 5 chunks in total, sorted by the original serial number.

(2) Also, **under separate cover** we are sending you a full range of samples.
(此外, 在另函中我们将会附上一个全方位的样品。)
(3) As requested, we now enclose our quotation sheet with samples and catalogues to be sent **under separate cover**.
(按照贵方要求, 我们现在附上我们的样品和产品目录报价表, 将在另函中发出。)
(4) In order to send you a rough idea of our products, we are airmailing you **under separate cover** a copy of our main items suppliable at present for your reference.
(为了使贵方对我方产品有大致的了解, 在另函中寄上目前我方主要可供货物的说明材料一份, 以供参考。)

In these example sentences, the original serial number of "under separate cover" is 88878, with a frequency of 4 in the corpus, and all of them are translated into "在另函中". Therefore, they are in complete correspondence, expressed as E88878 = C88878, where E88878 stands for "under separate cover" and C88878 for "在另函中"; the corresponding ratio is 100%, and the standard score is 100 (see Table 4.12).

The sentences containing the chunk with the original serial number 88933 (in bold) are listed as follows:

(1) The demand for LCD Monitors is brisk and we recommend you to send your order before the end of October. We await **with keen interest** your trial order.
(由于该液晶显示器的需求旺盛, 我们建议您在 10 月底之前发送订单。我们殷切期待您的试订单。)
(2) We sincerely hope that our request will meet with your approval and await your soonest reply **with keen interest**.
(我们真诚地希望我们的要求能得到您的同意, 并殷切期待您尽快回复。)
(3) We are very interested in an exclusive arrangement with your factory for the promotion of your products in Bahrain. We await your news **with keen interest**.
(盼能成为贵公司独家代理, 促销在巴林市场的货品。殷切期待早日回复。)
(4) We trust the above will be acceptable to you and await your trial order **with keen interest**.
(我们希望你方将接受上述订单, 殷切期待你方的试订单。)

In these example sentences, the original serial number of 88933, the chunk "with keen interest" appears 4 times in the corpus, and the Chinese versions are "殷切期待". Therefore, they are in complete correspondence. The corresponding rule is E88933 = C88933, where E88933 stands for "with keen interest" and C88933 for "殷切期待". The corresponding ratio is 100%, and the standard score is 100 (see Table 4.13).

Table 4.12 Corresponding rule and standard score of chunks with original serial number 88878

Original serial number	Chunk	Chinese translation	Corresponding rule	Standard score
88878	E88878 = under separate cover	C88878 = 在另函中	E88878 = C88878	100

Table 4.13 Corresponding rule and standard score of chunks with original serial number 88933

Original serial number	Chunk	Chinese translation	Corresponding rule	Standard score
88933	E88933 = with keen interest	C88933 = 殷切期待	E88933 = C88933	100

The sentences containing the chunk with the original serial number 102522 (in bold) are listed as follows:

(1) As the stipulated **time of shipments** is drawing near, please make the amendments to the L/C as soon as possible so that we can effect shipment in time.
(由于规定的装运时间临近，请尽快做出修订，让信用证尽快生效，以便我们可以及时装运。)
(2) Therefore, please inform us of CIF London price, discount, **time of shipment** and other details.
(因此，请告知我们伦敦的到岸价，折扣价，装运时间以及其他细节。)
(3) Payment: By confirmed, irrevocable L/C payable by draft at 60 days sight to be opened 30 days before the **time of shipment**.
(付款方式：凭保兑的、不可撤销的信用证支付，60天远期汇票在装运时间前 30 天开通。)
(4) Our usual terms of payment are by confirmed, irrevocable letter of credit for the full amount of the invoice value to be established in our favor, available by draft at sight, reaching us one month ahead of shipment, remaining valid for negotiation in China till the 21st day after the prescribed **time of shipment**, and allowing transshipment and partial shipment.
(我们的一贯付款条件是采用保兑的、不可撤销的、金额为发票的全部数额的、以我方为抬头人的即期信用证，于装运前一个月寄至我们。信用证在中国的议付有效期为规定的装运时间后 21 天止，且准许转船和分批装运。)
(5) While requesting you to expedite the establishment of your L/C, we have to ask for a corresponding extension of the **time of shipment**, which is necessary due to your delay in opening the credit.
(同时需要贵方加快不可撤销信用证的办理，我方不得不要求一个相应延期的装运时间，在开放信用证中由于贵方的耽误这是必要的。)

In these example sentences, the original serial number of "time of shipment" is 102522, and its frequency in the corpus is 5. It is found that the corresponding translations are all "装运时间", showing that it is a complete correspondence. The corresponding rule is E102522 = C102522, where E102522 stands for "time of shipment" and C102522 for "装运时间". The corresponding ratio is 100% and the standard score is 100 (see Table 4.14).

The sentences containing the chunk with the original serial number 114413 (in bold) are listed as follows:

Table 4.14 Corresponding rule and standard score of chunks with original serial number 102522

Original serial number	Chunk	Chinese translation	Corresponding rule	Standard score
102522	E102522 = time of shipment	C102522 = 装运时间	E102522 = C102522	100

(1) You **may rest assured** that we shall effect shipment with the least possible delay upon receipt of your credit.
(我方将竭力避免收到您的信用证后带来的延误装运, 敬请放心。)
(2) Meanwhile, you **may rest assured** that we shall effect shipment with no delay upon receipt of the L/C.
(同时, 一旦收到信用证, 我们将立即装运, 敬请放心。)
(3) You **may rest assured** that our shipment will meet your requirements in every respect.
(我们的货物将在各方面满足您的要求, 敬请放心。)
(4) You **may rest assured** that we shall make up your order upon receipt of the credit and effect the shipment within the time you requested.
(在贵方要求的时间内, 一旦收到信用票据, 我们就发送订货, 敬请放心。)

In the above examples, the original serial number of "may rest assured" is 114413, and its frequency in the corpus is 4. Since all of the translations are "敬请放心", they are in complete correspondence. The corresponding rule is E114413 = C114413, where E114413 stands for "may rest assured" and C114413 for "敬请放心". The corresponding ratio is 100% and the standard score is 100 (see Table 4.15).

The sentences containing the chunk with the original serial number 132113 (in bold) are listed as follows:

(1) We can **supply from stock** and will have no trouble in meeting your delivery date.
(我们可以提供现货并按你方所定的日期交货。)
(2) If you can **supply from stock** we are prepared to order 100,000 yards for shipment to be made as early as possible by direct steamer to Hong Kong.
(如果你能提供现货, 我们准备以 10 万码作为条件尽早通过直接轮船来香港。)
(3) Please send us particulars of any models you recommend and **supply from stock**.
(请给我们发来你们推荐和能够提供现货的样品资料。)

Table 4.15 Corresponding rule and standard score of chunks with original serial number 114413

Original serial number	Chunk	Chinese translation	Corresponding rule	Standard score
114413	E114413 = may rest assured	C114413 = 敬请放心	E114413 = C114413	100

Table 4.16 Corresponding rule and standard score of chunks with original serial number 132113

Original serial number	Chunk	Chinese translation	Corresponding rule	Standard score
132113	E132113 = supply from stock	C132113 = 提供现货	E132113 = C132113	100

In these example sentences, the original serial number of "supply from stock" is 132113, and its frequency is 3. The Chinese translations are all "提供现货". Therefore, they are in complete correspondence, and the corresponding rule is E132113 = C132113, where E132113 stands for "supply from stock" and C132113 for "提供现货". The corresponding ratio is 100% and the standard score is 100 (see Table 4.16).

c. Four-word chunks[3]

The sentences containing the chunk with the original serial number 17093 (in bold) are listed as follows:

(1) As we are in urgent need of these goods, we hope you will make delivery **at an early date.**
(由于我们对这些产品的迫切需求, 我们希望您早日交付。)
(2) We hope you will give our suggestion your most favorable consideration and let us have your decision **at an early date.**
(我们希望你们能对我们的建议给予认真的考虑，并早日让我们知道你们的决定。)
(3) Please confirm your order soon so that you and your customers will enjoy the fine quality and reliable after-sale service of our products **at an early date.**
(请尽快确认您的订单，方便您和您的客户早日感受我们上好的品质和可靠的售后服务。)
(4) We look forward to your settlement **at an early date.**
(我方期待着贵方早日解决这一问题。)
(5) As we are in urgent need of these goods, we hope you will make delivery **at an early date.**
(由于我们对这些产品的迫切需求, 我们希望您早日交付。)
(6) If you think our proposal acceptable, please let us have your order **at an early date.**
(如认为我方报盘可以接受, 请早日下单。)
(7) We have owed your address to the Commercial Counselor of your Embassy in New York and are now writing to you for the establishment of business relations in the scope of light industry merchandises **at an early date.**
(我们从你方纽约大使馆商务参赞处得知贵公司地址, 现特致函给贵方, 以期早日在轻工业产品方面建立业务关系。)
(8) We hope to receive your specific enquiry **at an early date.**
(我们希望早日收到你方的具体询价单。)

[3] There are 5 chunks in total, sorted by the original serial number.

(9) We trust you will open the relative L/C in our favor **at an early date.**
(我方相信你方会早日开出以我方为受益人的相关信用证。)

In examples above, the original serial number is 17093, the frequency of "at an early date" is 9. It is found that the Chinese translations are all "早日", showing that they are in complete correspondence. The corresponding rule is E17093 = C17093, where E17093 stands for "at an early date" and C17093 for "早日". The corresponding ratio is 100%, which could be converted to the standard score 100 (see Table 4.17).

The sentences containing the chunk with the original serial number 73731 (in bold) are listed as follows:

(1) Therefore, we should ask you to take immediate action to have the L/C established so that we may execute the order **within the contracted time.**
(因此, 我们请您立即采取行动开立信用证, 以便我们可以在合同规定期内履行订单。)
(2) We must insist on delivery **within the contracted time** and reserve the right to reject the goods if we fail to receive the goods before this week.
(我方坚持在合同规定期内装运, 如果在本周以前我方仍未能收到这批货物, 我方将保留退货的权力。)
(3) We will, however, do everything possible to ensure that the goods are shipped **within the contracted time.**
(然而, 本公司可确保该货将在合同规定期内送抵。)

In these example sentences, the original serial number of "within the contracted time" is 73731, and its frequency is 3 in the corpus. It is found that its Chinese translations are all "在合同规定期内". Therefore, they are in complete correspondence, and the corresponding rule is E73731 = C73731, where E73731 stands for "within the contracted time" and C73731 for "在合同规定期内". The corresponding ratio is 100% and the standard score is 100 (see Table 4.18).

The sentences containing the chunk with the original serial number 83853 (in bold) are listed as follows:

Table 4.17 Corresponding rule and standard score of chunks with original serial number 17093

Original serial number	Chunk	Chinese translation	Corresponding rule	Standard score
17093	E17093 = at an early date	C17093 = 早日	E17093 = C17093	100

Table 4.18 Corresponding rule and standard score of chunks with original serial number 73731

Original serial number	Chunk	Chinese translation	Corresponding rule	Standard score
73731	E73731 = within the contracted time	C73731 = 在合同规定期内	E73731 = C73731	100

(1) Our present difficulty is purely temporary. Before the **end of this month** payments are due to us from a number of our regular customers who are notably prompt payers.
(我们目前的困难纯粹是暂时性的, 在本月底前我公司客户账目到期缴清, 那些老客户都是准时结账者。)

(2) We were under the impression that payment was not due until the **end of this month**, when we would have no difficulty in settling our account.
(我们误以为账款至本月底才到期缴付, 那时结算并无困难。)

(3) Having carefully considered your letter of 7th March we have decided to allow you to defer payment of your account to the **end of this month**.
(关于 3 月 7 日来信, 经慎重考虑, 我们决定将贵方的付款期限放宽至本月底。)

(4) You invoice No. 342 for 5,000 RMB worth of goods supplied on 4th May is due for payment at the **end of this month**.
(5 月 4 日供应的价值人民币 5000 元的货物, 是由您第 342 号发票发出, 并定于本月底结账。)

(5) This loan is due for repayment at the **end of this month** and I had already taken steps to prepare for this, but unfortunately, due to a fire at my warehouse a fortnight ago, I have been faced with heavy unexpected payments.
(该笔贷款将于本月底到期, 本公司也准备还款。然而不幸的是, 两星期前本公司货仓失火, 导致本公司遭受巨大损失。)

(6) Please guarantee dispatch in time to reach us by the **end of this month**.
(请贵方保证能及时交货, 使我们于本月底收到。)

(7) On 10th February last I ordered one hundred swimming trousers, to be delivered at the **end of this month**.
(在 2 月 10 日, 我最后一次订购游泳裤 100 条, 预定在本月底交货。)

(8) The policy is being prepared accordingly and will be presented to you by the **end of this month** together with our debit note for the premium.
(该政策是据此编写, 并将在本月底与保险费的缴费单一并提交给您。)

(9) We will expect your consignment by the **end of this month**.
(我们期待你方至本月底能发货。)

(10) We are very interested in the different types of watches you offer and have decided to place a trail order for the following, on the terms stated in your letter, but only if you can guarantee dispatch in time to reach us by the **end of this month**.
(我公司对您提供的各种手表很感兴趣。根据信内的条件, 我们决定试订下列货品, 但需要贵公司保证在本月底及时运到。)

(11) In your letter of 6th August you ask us to cancel part of the order you placed on 10th February for swimming trousers to be delivered at the **end of this month**.
(您 8 月 6 日来信, 要求取消在 2 月 10 日所下的部分游泳裤订单, 该批货物原定在本月底装箱发货。)

In these example sentences, the original serial number of "end of this month" is 83853, and it appears 11 times in the corpus. We find that all of its translations are "本月月底", so they are in complete correspondence. The corresponding rule is E83853

= C83853, where E83853 stands for "end of this month" and C83853 for "本月月底". The corresponding ratio is 100% and the standard score is 100 (see Table 4.19).

The sentences containing the chunk with the original serial number 101893 (in bold) are listed as follows:

(1) Meanwhile, in order to **avoid subsequent amendments**, please make sure that the UC stipulations should be in exact accordance with the terms of the Contract. (同时, 为了避免日后修改, 请确保加州规定与合同上的条款保持绝对一致。)
(2) And in the meantime, please see to it that the L/C stipulations are in strict conformity with those of the confirmation to **avoid subsequent amendments** of discrepancies in the L/C.
(同时, 请确保信用证中的条款严格符合确认书中的, 以避免日后修改信用证中的差异。)
(3) Meanwhile, please see to it that the stipulations in the relative credit should strictly conform to the terms in our sales confirmation in order to **avoid subsequent amendments**.
(同时， 请确保相关信贷规定严格按照我方的销售确认条款以避免日后修改。)

In these example sentences, the original serial number of "avoid subsequent amendments" is 101893, and its frequency in the corpus is 3. It is found that the corresponding translations are all "避免日后修改". Therefore, they are in complete correspondence. The corresponding rule is E101893 = C101893, where E101893 stands for "avoid subsequent amendments" and C101893 for "避免日后修改". The corresponding ratio is 100% and the standard score is 100 (see Table 4.20).

The sentences containing the chunk with the original serial number 127043 (in bold) are listed as follows:

(1) With the best will in the world to serve you, we are afraid it would be neither worth your while, nor ours, to continue business **on a cash basis**.

Table 4.19 Corresponding rule and standard score of chunks with original serial number 83853

Original serial number	Chunk	Chinese translation	Corresponding rule	Standard score
83853	E83853 = end of this month	C83853 = 本月底	E83853 = C83853	100

Table 4.20 Corresponding rule and standard score of chunks with original serial number 101893

Original serial number	Chunk	Chinese translation	Corresponding rule	Standard score
101893	E101893 = avoid subsequent amendments	C101893 = 避免日后修改	E101893 = C101893	100

Table 4.21 Corresponding rule and standard score of chunks with original serial number 127043

Original serial number	Chunk	Chinese translation	Corresponding rule	Standard score
127043	E127043 = on a cash basis	C127043 = 现金方式	E127043 = C127043	100

(对你我而言，如继续以现金方式交易，结果都是不值得的，即使我公司非常愿意为您服务，也是徒然。)

(2) Not a few get into difficulties because they over commit themselves before they are thoroughly established, and although we believe that your own business promises well, we think it would be better for you to make your purchases **on a cash basis** for the present.
(很多新成立的公司在还没有完全建立好基础之前便发生问题，这是因为过度发展超过本身能力所致。虽然本公司深信您的业务会有良好的前景，但认为暂以现金方式购货对您更为有利。)

(3) We do business **on a cash basis**, so we can not supply you with goods on credit.
(我们以现金方式交易，所以不能用赊贷方式供货。)

(4) As the urgency of your order left no time to make the usual enquiries, we are compelled to place this transaction **on a cash basis** and have drawn on you through Credit Bank Ltd. for the amount of the enclosed invoice. The bank will instruct their correspondent in Sydney to pass the bill of lading to you against payment of the draft.
(由于贵公司的订单是如此急迫，以至于本公司无暇查询，因此本公司不得已要求现金方式交易，并且已通过信用银行有限公司向您提取账款，该行将通知悉尼的分行，将提货单交给您。)

In these example sentences, the original serial number of "on a cash basis" is 127043, with a frequency of 4. We find that all of its translations are "现金方式", indicating a complete correspondence. The corresponding rule is E127043 = C127043, where E127043 stands for "on a cash basis" and C127043 for "现金方式". The corresponding ratio is 100% and the standard score is 100 (see Table 4.21).

d. Five-word chunks[4]

The sentences containing the chunk with the original serial number 132443 (in bold) are listed as follows:

(1) We are enclosing our illustrated catalogue giving the details you ask for and also under separate cover sending you **a full range of samples**.
(我们随函寄去带有插图的目录，其中有你们想要的详细资料，在另函中还邮寄去一整套样品。)

(2) Also, under separate cover we are sending you **a full range of samples**.
① There are 10 chunks in total, sorted by the original serial number.
(此外，在另函中我们将送上一整套样品。)

[4] There are 2 chunks in total, sorted by the original serial number.

(3) I have informed them that you will call on them during next week with **a full range of samples.**
(我已通知该公司, 说您将于下星期携带一整套样品拜访他们。)

The original serial number of "a full range of samples" is 132443, and its frequency in the corpus is 3. It is found that all of its translations are "一整套样品". Therefore, they are in complete correspondence, and the corresponding rule is E132443 = C132443, where E132443 stands for "a full range of samples" and C132443 for "一整套样品". The corresponding ratio is 100% and the standard score is 100 (see Table 4.22).

The sentences containing the chunk with the original serial number 135741 (in bold) are listed as follows:

(1) Whatever the reason, we are keen on receiving your **reply at your earliest convenience** so that we can make timely arrangement to improve the quality and related service of our products.
(无论哪种原因, 我们热切期望您方便时尽早回复, 以便我们及时做出安排, 改进产品的质量与相关服务。)
(2) Kindly let us have your **reply at your earliest convenience**.
(请在您方便时尽早回复。)
(3) I sincerely hope that you will take my advice into consideration, and I look forward to your **reply at your earliest convenience**.
(我真诚地希望您能仔细考虑我的建议, 并期望您方便时尽早回复。)

In these example sentences, the original serial number of "reply at your earliest convenience" is 135741 with a frequency of 3. The corresponding Chinese translations are all "方便时尽早回复". Therefore, they are in complete correspondence, and the corresponding rule is E135741 = C135741, where E135741 stands for "reply at your earliest convenience" and C135741 for "方便时尽早回复". The corresponding ratio is 100%, and the standard score is 100 (see Table 4.23).

Table 4.22 Corresponding rule and standard score of chunks with original serial number 132443

Original serial number	Chunk	Chinese translation	Corresponding rule	Standard score
132443	E132443 = a full range of samples	C132443 = 一整套样品	E132443 = C132443	100

Table 4.23 Corresponding rule and standard score of chunks with original serial number 135741

Original serial number	Chunk	Chinese translation	Corresponding rule	Standard score
135741	E135741 = reply at your earliest convenience	C135741 = 方便时尽早回复	E135741 = C135741	100

Table 4.24 Corresponding rule and standard score of chunks with original serial number 2529

Original serial number	Chunk	Chinese translation	Corresponding rule	Standard score
2529	E2529 = lead to further business between us	C2529 = 促使我们之间的进一步合作	E2529 = C2529	100

e. Six-word chunks[5]

The sentences containing the chunk with the original serial number 2529 (in bold) are listed as follows:

(1) I hope our handling of this order will **lead to further business between us** and to a happy and lasting association.
(希望这宗订单的处理能促使我们之间的进一步合作，并借此建立一个长久和愉快的联系。)
(2) We are enclosing a copy of our catalogue and hope that this initial order will **lead to further business between us**.
(我方特随函附上一份产品目录，希望该初始订单能促使我们之间的进一步合作。)
(3) We hope that our handling of your first order will **lead to further business between us** and mark the beginning of good working relationship.
(希望对贵方第一个订单的处理能促使我们之间的进一步合作，并成为双方良好工作关系开始的标志。)

In these example sentences, the original serial number of "lead to further business between us" is 2529, with a frequency of 3. We find that the Chinese translations are all "促使我们之间的进一步合作". Therefore, they are in complete correspondence. The corresponding rule is E2529 = C2529, where E2529 stands for "lead to further business between us" and C2529 for "促使我们之间的进一步合作". The corresponding ratio is 100% and the standard score is 100 (see Table 4.24).

The sentences containing the chunk with the original serial number 117328 (in bold) are listed as follows:

(1) We are **enclosing a copy of our catalogue** and hope that this initial order will lead to further business between us.
(我方特随函附上一份产品目录，希望该初始订单能促使我们之间的进一步合作。)
(2) As you may not be aware of the wide range of the goods we deal in. We are **enclosing a copy of our catalogue** and look forward to your repeat orders.
(也许贵公司可能没有意识到我方大范围的货物处理，现随函附上一份产品目录, 并期待您的再次订购。)
(3) As you may not be aware of the wide range of goods we deal in, we are **enclosing a copy of our catalogue** and hope that our handing of your first order with us

[5] There are 2 chunks in total, sorted by the original serial number.

Table 4.25 Corresponding rule and standard score of chunks with original serial number 117328

Original serial number	Chunk	Chinese translation	Corresponding rule	Standard score
117328	E117328 = enclosing a copy of our catalogue	C117328 = 随函附上一份产品目录	E117328 = C117328	100

will lead to further business between us and mark the beginning of a happy working relationship.
(您也许对我公司经营的货物范围不太了解, 现随函附上一份产品目录, 希望自第一个订单开始, 彼此建立更多的业务来往, 展开愉快的工作关系。)

In these example sentences, the original serial number of 117328, the chunk "enclosing a copy of our catalogue" appears three times in the corpus. It is found that all of its translations are "随函附上一份产品目录", indicating a complete correspondence. The corresponding rule is E117328 = C117328, where E117328 stands for "enclosing a copy of our catalogue" and C117328 for "随函附上一份产品目录". The corresponding ratio is 100% and the standard score is 100 (see Table 4.25).

f. Seven-word chunks[6]

The sentences containing the chunk with the original serial number 48722 (in bold) are listed as follows:

(1) We believe that the solution we have made will satisfy you and **look forward to receiving your further orders**.
(但愿我方的处理意见能使贵方满意, 并期望得到贵方更多的订单。)
(2) We hope that the arrangement we have made will satisfy you and **your further orders**.
(我方希望我们的行动安排能满足贵方, 并期望得到贵方更多的订单。)
(3) We appreciate your cooperation and look forward to receiving your further orders.
(我们非常感谢您的合作并期望得到贵方更多的订单。)

In these example sentences, the original serial number of "look forward to receiving your further orders" is 48722, with a frequency of 3 in the corpus. All of the corresponding translations are "期望得到贵方更多的订单". Therefore, they are in complete correspondence, and the corresponding rule is E48722 = C48722, where E48722 stands for "look forward to receiving your further orders" and C48722 for "期望得到贵方更多的订单". The corresponding ratio is 100% and the standard score is 100 (see Table 4.26).

The sentences containing the chunk with the original serial number 96055 (in bold) are listed as follows:

[6] There are 2 chunks in total, sorted by the original serial number.

Table 4.26 Corresponding rule and standard score of chunks with original serial number 48722

Original serial number	Chunk	Chinese translation	Corresponding rule	Standard score
48722	E48722 = look forward to receiving your further orders	C48722 = 期望得到贵方更多的订单	E48722 = C48722	100

Table 4.27 Corresponding rule and standard score of chunks with original serial number 96055

Original serial number	Chunk	Chinese translation	Corresponding rule	Standard score
96055	E96055 = do not hesitate to let us know	C96055 = 毫不犹豫地告诉我们	E96055 = C96055	100

(1) If you find any defect in our last shipment, please **do not hesitate to let us know**.
(如果您发现在我们的最后装运有任何缺陷, 请毫不犹豫地告诉我们。)
(2) If any of the items illustrated in the booklet interests you, please **do not hesitate to let us know**.
(如果您对我们上述产品册中的新项目感兴趣, 请毫不犹豫地告诉我们。)
(3) If possible, please **do not hesitate to let us know** your detailed requirements.
(如果可能的话, 请毫不犹豫地告诉我们您的详细要求。)

In these example sentences, the original serial number of "do not hesitate to let us know" is 96055, and its frequency in the corpus is 3. We find that the Chinese translations are all "毫不犹豫地告诉我们", indicating a complete correspondence. The corresponding rule is E96055 = C96055, where E96055 stands for "do not hesitate to let us know" and C96055 stands for "毫不犹豫地告诉我们". The corresponding ratio is 100%, and the standard score is 100 (see Table 4.27).

g. Eight-word chunks[7]

The sentences containing the chunk with the original serial number 25398 (in bold) are listed as follows:

(1) As it is said that you are looking for a partner in the field of car parts, I am writing to ask if you would **be willing to establish business relations with us**.
(听说贵公司正在寻找有关汽车配件的合作者，我特此致信询问贵方是否愿意与我们建立业务关系。)
(2) We have obtained your name and address from Far East Electronic Company and we are writing to enquire whether you would **be willing to establish business relations with us**.

[7] There are 2 chunks in total, sorted by the original serial number.

(我们从远东电子公司得知贵司商号与地址,特此来函,贵公司是否愿意与我们建立业务关系。)

(3) We are e-mailing you to enquire whether you would **be willing to** establish business relations with us.
(这封邮件想咨询您是否愿意与我们建立业务关系。)

In these example sentences, the original serial number of "be willing to establish business relations with us" is 25398, with a frequency of 3. All of the translations are "愿意与我们建立业务关系". Therefore, they are in complete correspondence, and the corresponding rule is E25398 = C25398, where E25398 stands for "be willing to establish business relations with us" and C25398 for "愿意与我们建立业务关系". The corresponding ratio is 100% and the standard score is 100 (see Table 4.28).

The sentences containing the chunk with the original serial number 117310 (in bold) are listed as follows:

(1) As you may not be aware of **the wide range of goods we deal in**.
(贵方可能不知我方的商品交易范围。)
(2) As you may not be aware of **the wide range of the goods we deal in**. We are enclosing a copy of our catalogue and look forward to your repeat orders.
(也许贵公司可能没有意识到我方的商品交易范围, 现随函附上一份我们的产品目录,并期待您的再次订购。)
(3) As you may not be aware of **the wide range of goods we deal in**, we are enclosing a copy of our catalogue and hope that our handing of your first order with us will lead to further business between us and mark the beginning of a happy working relationship.
(您也许对我方的商品交易范围不太了解,现附上目录一份,希望对贵方第一个订单的处理能促使我们之间的进一步合作, 并成为双方良好工作关系开始的标志。)

In these example sentences, with the original serial number of 117310, the chunk "the wide range of goods we deal in" appears 3 times in the corpus. We find that the corresponding translations are all "我方的商品交易范围", showing a complete correspondence, and the corresponding rule is E117310 = C117310, where E117310 stands for "the wide range of goods we deal in" and C117310 for "我方的商品交易范围". The corresponding ratio is 100% and the standard score is 100 (see Table 4.29).

Table 4.28 Corresponding rule and standard score of chunks with original serial number 25398

Original serial number	Chunk	Chinese translation	Corresponding rule	Standard score
25398	E25398 = be willing to establish business relations with us	C25398 = 愿意与我们建立业务关系	E25398 = C25398	100

Table 4.29 Corresponding rule and standard score of chunks with original serial number 117310

Original serial number	Chunk	Chinese translation	Corresponding rule	Standard score
117310	E117310 = the wide range of goods we deal in	C117310 = 我方的商品交易范围	E117310 = C117310	100

Table 4.30 Corresponding rule and standard score of chunks with original serial number 21108

Original serial number	Chunk	Chinese translation	Corresponding rule	Standard score
21108	E21108 = which the port of destination and our order number	C21108 = 其……目的港和订单号码	E21108 = C21108	100

h. Nine-word chunks[8]

The sentences containing the chunk with the original serial number 21108 (in bold) are listed as follows:

(1) On the outer packing please mark our initials CCO, under **which the port of destination and our order number** should be stenciled.
(请在外包装上注明我方的首字母 CCO, 其下应印刷目的港和订单号码。)
(2) On the outer packing please mark our initials ABC, under **which the port of destination and our order number** should be stenciled.
(请在外包装上注明我方的首字母 ABC, 其中规定, 目的港和订单号码应该有钢印。)
(3) On the outer packing please mark our initials SCC, under **which the port of destination and our order number** should be stenciled.
(请在外包装上注明我方的首字母 SCC, 其下面应印刷目的港和订单号码。)

In these example sentences, the original serial number of "which the port of destination and our order number" is 21108, and its frequency is 3. It is found that the corresponding Chinese translations are all "其……目的港和订单号码". Therefore, they are in complete correspondence, and the corresponding rule could be written as E21108 = C21108, where E21108 stands for "which the port of destination and our order number" and C21108 for "其……目的港和订单号码". The corresponding ratio is 100% and the standard score is 100 (see Table 4.30).

The sentences containing the chunk with the original serial number 90087 (in bold) are listed as follows[9]:

[8] There are 2 chunks in total, sorted by the original serial number.
[9] The following three examples are from different English letters.

(1) We are **indeed sorry that you found our price too high**.
(我们真是遗憾您觉得我们的价格太高。)
(2) We are **indeed sorry that you found our price too high**.
(我们真是遗憾您觉得我们的价格太高。)
(3) We are **indeed sorry that you found our price too high**.
(我们真是遗憾您觉得我们的价格太高。)

In these example sentences, the original serial number of "indeed sorry that you found our price too high" is 90087, and its frequency is 3. We find that all of the Chinese translations are "真是遗憾您觉得我们的价格太高". Therefore, they are in complete correspondence, and the corresponding rule is E90087 = C90087, where E90087 stands for "indeed sorry that you found our price too high" and C90087 for "真是遗憾您觉得我们的价格太高". The corresponding ratio is 100% and the standard score is 100 (see Table 4.31).

B. Incomplete correspondence and its corresponding rules

Through the analysis of example sentences in the parallel corpus, it is found that 17 MT-oriented corresponding chunks in English-Chinese business letters are in incomplete correspondence. In this part, the incomplete correspondences and corresponding rules as well as the standard scores are explained according to the original serial number.

The sentences containing the chunk with the original serial number 42463 (in bold) are listed as follows:

(1) Considering the quality of the goods offered we do not feel that the prices we quoted are at all excessive, but bearing in mind the special character of trade, we have decided to offer you a **special discount** of 3% on a first order of H. K. $4,000.
(从所供货物质量来考虑, 我们并不认为定价过高, 但考虑到交易的特殊情况, 决定首宗 4000 港元的订单给予 3%的特别折扣。)
(2) We shall allow you **a special discount** of 4% provided your order call for a minimum quantity of 6,000 dozen.
(只要订单起订量达到 6000 打, 我们允许 4%的特殊折扣。)
(3) In view of the good quality and the rising prices of raw materials, we do not feel that the prices we quoted are at all excessive, but bearing in mind the special character of your trade, we have decided to offer you a **special discount** of 5% on a first order for 5,000.

Table 4.31 Corresponding rule and standard score of chunks with original serial number 90087

Original serial number	Chunk	Chinese translation	Corresponding rule	Standard score
90087	E90087 = indeed sorry that you found our price too high	C90087 = 真是遗憾您觉得我们的价格太高	E90087 = C90087	100

(由于良好的商品质量和原材料价格上涨,我们不认为我们的报价过高。但是我们考虑到与你方的特殊的贸易关系,我们已经决定,如果你方的第一次订单达 5000 件,我们将给予你方 5%的特别折扣。)

(4) You are already aware of our terms of business, but to encourage you to lay in a stock of the new tubeless FLYING DEER. We will allow a **special discount** of 5% on any order received on or before 31st May.
(为了使贵公司可以在新飞无内胎飞鹿股市中获益更多,我们将对 5. 月 31 日之前收到的任何订单提供 5%的特别折扣。)

In these example sentences, the original serial number of "special discount" is 42463, with a frequency 4. We find that the Chinese translations of sentences (1), (3) and (4) are all "特别折扣", while that of sentence (2) is "特殊折扣". Therefore, they are in incomplete correspondence. Corresponding rule ① is E42463 ≈ C42463a, where E42463 stands for "special discount" and C42463a for "特别折扣"; the corresponding ratio is 75%, or the standard score of 75. Corresponding rule ② is E42463 ≈ C42463b, where C42463b stands for "特殊折扣"; the corresponding ratio is 25%, converted to the standard score of 25 (see Table 4.32).

The sentences containing the chunk with the original serial number 46811 (in bold) are listed as follows:

(1) I am sorry not to be able to grant your request of 20th July for an overdraft against personal security but, realizing how helpful a short-term credit would be to you, the bank would be prepared to consider an overdraft over the period you mention if you could **provide a guarantor**.
(非常抱歉,本银行不能满足贵公司 7 月 20 日提出的以私人保证透支的请求。但看到短期借贷会对贵公司有所帮助,若您能提供担保人的话,银行方面会考虑给予透支。)

(2) If you can **provide a guarantor** as suggested, please get in touch with me again and I will arrange to discuss the matter with you in detail.
(如贵公司有可能提供担保人的话,请再与本银行联络,届时本银行一定安排与贵公司详细讨论有关事宜。)

(3) To some extent your offer to act in a delcredere capacity meets our objections and for a trial period we are prepared to accept it on the terms stated, namely an extra commission of 3%, provided you are willing, either to **provide a guarantor** acceptable to us, or to lodge adequate security with our bankers.

Table 4.32 Corresponding rule and standard score of chunks with original serial number 42463

Original serial number	Chunk	Chinese translation	Corresponding rule	Standard score
42463	E42463 = special discount	C42463a = 特别折扣	① E42463 ≈ C42463a	75
		C42463b = 特殊折扣	② E42463 ≈ C42463b	25

(贵公司应允提供保证收取货款, 在一定程度上符合本公司的目的。本公司准备接受该建议, 试用一段时期。附带条款是另加佣金 3%, 并需要您愿意提供我公司可接受的担保人, 或在我公司银行存储足够保证金。)

In these example sentences, the original serial number of "provide a guarantor" is 46811, and its frequency in the corpus is 3. The corresponding Chinese translations of sentences (1) and (2) are both "提供担保人" whereas that of sentence (3) is "提供……担保人", indicating an incomplete correspondence. Corresponding rule ① is E46811 ≈ C46811a, where E46811 stands for "provide a guarantor" and C46811a for "提供担保人"; the corresponding rate is 67% and the standard score is 67. Corresponding rule ② is E46811 ≈ C46811b, where C46811b stands for "提供……担保人"; the corresponding rate is 33% and the standard score is 33 (see Table 4.33).

The sentences containing the chunk with the original serial number 58930 (in bold) are listed as follows:

(1) Enclosed please find a full set of **shipping documents** as required in your L/C No. 11000.
(随函附上贵方 11000 号信用证中所要求的一整套货运文件。)
(2) In keeping with our usual terms of payment we have drawn on you at 60 days and passed the draft and **shipping documents** to our bankers.
(依照一贯的付款条件, 60 天内向贵公司提款, 现已将汇票及货运文件送交我们的银行。)
(3) Since the standing of this company is unknown to us, we do not wish to hand over the **shipping documents** against their mere acceptance of a bill of exchange.
(由于我公司对该公司资金情况不大了解, 因此不愿意只收到该公司汇票, 就送上货运文件。)
(4) Please ensure that we'll get correct **shipping documents** before the arrival of the goods.
(请确保在货物到达前我方可拿到正确的货运文件。)
(5) We are pleased to have received the **shipping documents** in due course and taken delivery of the goods on arrival of the S.S. "Princess" in Shanghai.
(我们很高兴及时收到贵方货运文件, 并已指派 "公主"号货轮在上海交货。)
(6) In addition to the ordinary **shipping documents**, please also submit certificate of origin for each shipment.
(除了普通的货运文件外, 也请提交每批货物的产地证书。)

Table 4.33 Corresponding rule and standard score of chunks with original serial number 46811

Original serial number	Chunk	Chinese translation	Corresponding rule	Standard score
46811	E46811 = provide a guarantor	C46811a = 提供担保人	① E46811 ≈ C46811a	67
		C46811b = 提供……担保人	② E46811 ≈ C46811b	33

(7) We will send you bill of lading and other **shipping documents** as soon as we receive them and meanwhile enclose a proforma invoice showing prices at which the goods should be offered for sale.
(我公司一旦收到提货单及其他货运文件, 当即寄给您。同时, 我公司寄上售货形式发票一张, 上面将注明销售价格。)
(8) We usually accept payment by irrevocable letter of credit payable against **shipping documents**.
(我们通常只接受不可撤销的信用证, 凭货运单据付款。)
(9) You should send one copy of the **shipping documents** to the port of destination together with the shipment.
(装船同时贵方应将货运单据副本寄送目的港。)
(10) I also sent you the relevant **shipping documents** by fax. Please check.
(相关货运单据也已经传真给您, 请注意查收。)

In these example sentences, the original serial number of "shipping documents" is 58930, with a frequency of 10 in the corpus. The corresponding translations of sentences (1)–(7) are all "货运文件", while those of the example sentences (8)–(10) are "货运单据". Therefore, they are in incomplete correspondence. Corresponding rule ① is E58930 ≈ C58930a, where E58930 stands for "shipping documents" and C58930a for "货运文件"; the corresponding ratio is 70% and the standard score is 70. Corresponding rule ② is E58930 ≈ C58930b, where C58930b stands for "货运单据"; the corresponding ratio is 30% and the standard score is 30 (see Table 4.34).

The sentences containing the chunk with the original serial number 66000 (in bold) are listed as follows:

(1) **Please let me know** if you would like additional copies of this booklet and of the materials that were handed out at the convention.
(如果你想得到我们在公约上发放的小册子和材料的额外副本, 请告知我。)
(2) In addition, would you like to transport our goods by train or by boat? Please let me know about the details of the type of conveyance and freight.
(另外, 贵方是要用火车运输还是船运呢?请告知我关于运输方式和运费的相关事宜。)
(3) **Please let me know** after you decide.
(您决定后请告知我。)
(4) Will you **please let me know** either by letter or by telephone whether you will be free to come.

Table 4.34 Corresponding rule and standard score of chunks with original serial number 58930

Original serial number	Chunk	Chinese translation	Corresponding rule	Standard score
58930	E58930 = shipping documents	C58930a = 货运文件	① E58930 ≈ C58930a	70
		C58930b = 货运单据	② E58930 ≈ C58930b	30

(请您以书信或电话告知我能否抽空前来。)

In these example sentences, the original serial number of "please let me know" is 66000, and its frequency in the corpus is 4. The Chinese translations of sentences (1)–(3) are "请告知我" while that of sentence (4) is "请……告知我". Therefore, it is an incomplete correspondence. Corresponding rule ① is E66000 ≈ C66000a, where E66000 stands for "please let me know" and C66000a for "请告知我"; the corresponding ratio is 75% and the standard score is 75. Corresponding rule ② is E66000 ≈ C66000b, where C66000b stands for "请……告知我"; the corresponding rate is 25% and the standard score is 25 (see Table 4.35).

The sentences containing the chunk with the original serial number 77426 (in bold) are listed as follows:

(1) As soon as **the said license is approved**, an L/C will be opened in your favor. Your full cooperation in this respect will be appreciated.
(一旦该许可获得批准, 将会为您开一张信用卡。我们对您在这一方面的全面合作将不胜感激。)
(2) After **the said license is approved**, an L/C will be opened in your favor. We would also like to act as your sole agent in Indian market.
(当该许可获得批准后, 一个信用证将会以你方为受益人开出。我方也希望担任贵公司在印度市场的唯一代理商。)
(3) After **the said license is approved**, we shall establish an irrevocable letter of credit in your favor. We hope it will be the first of many orders we will be placing with you.

(上述许可获得批准后， 我们将如您所愿建立一个不可撤销信用证。我们希望此次合作会成为以后订立众多订单的良好开端。)

In these example sentences, the original serial number of "the said license is approved" is 77426, and its frequency is 3. The Chinese translations of the sentences (1) and (2) are "该许可获得批准", while that of the sentence (3) is "上述许可获得批准", indicating an incomplete correspondence. Corresponding rule ① is E77426 ≈ C77426a, where E77426 stands for "the said license is approved" and C77426a for "该许可获得批准"; the corresponding rate is 67% and the standard score is 67. Corresponding rule ② is E77426 ≈ C77426b, where C77426b stands for "上述许可获得批准"; the corresponding rate is 33% and the standard score is 33 (see Table 4.36).

The sentences containing the chunk with the original serial number 83754 (in bold) are listed as follows:

Table 4.35 Corresponding rule and standard score of chunks with original serial number 66000

Original serial number	Chunk	Chinese translation	Corresponding rule	Standard score
66000	E66000 = please let me know	C66000a = 请告知我	① E66000 ≈ C66000a	75
		C66000b = 请……告知我	② E66000 ≈ C66000b	25

Table 4.36 Corresponding rule and standard score of chunks with original serial number 77426

Original serial number	Chunk	Chinese translation	Corresponding rule	Standard score
77426	E77426 = the said license is approved	C77426a = 该许可获得批准	① E77426 ≈ C77426a	67
		C77426b = 上述许可获得批准	② E77426 ≈ C77426b	33

(1) As stipulated, the shipping date is approaching and we should have received your **shipping advice**.
(按规定, 发货日期将近, 我方应已收到贵方的装运通知。)
(2) We look forward to receiving your **shipping advice**, by fax, within the next seven days.
(烦请于七天内将贵公司的装运通知传真给我方。)
(3) The seller should send by fax the **shipping advice** upon completion of shipment.
(一旦货物装船完毕, 卖方应立即传真装运通知。)
(4) On receiving your credit from the bank we will make up your order and will send **shipping advice** as soon as the shipment is completed.
(从银行收到您的信用卡后, 我们将弥补您的订单, 完成装运后将发出装运通知。)
(5) We look forward to receiving your **shipping advice**, by fax, within the next five days.
(烦请于五天内传真贵公司的装运通知。)
(6) For your information, this consignment will be shipped by S.S. "Hope" due to sail on or about June 10th. We shall send you the **shipping advice** in due course.
(您需要注意的是, 这批货将由"希望"号运送, 因为约 6 月 10 日起运, 我们将适时向贵方发出装运通知。)
(7) We look forward to receiving your **shipping advice** and thank you in advance.
(我们期待着您的装运通知, 并提前感谢。)
(8) We shall appreciate your close cooperation in this respect and await your **shipping advice**.
(我们将非常感谢您在这方面紧密合作, 期待您的装船通知。)

In these example sentences, the original serial number of "shipping advice" is 83754, with a frequency of 8. The Chinese translations of sentences (1)–(7) are all "装运通知", while that of sentence (8) is "装船通知". Therefore, they are incomplete correspondence. Corresponding rule ① is E83754 ≈ C83754a, where E83754 stands for "shipping advice" and C83754a for "装运通知"; the corresponding ratio is 88% and the standard score is 88. Corresponding rule ② is E83754 ≈ C83754b, where C83754b stands for "装船通知"; the corresponding rate is 12% and the standard score is 12 (see Table 4.37).

The sentences containing the chunk with the original serial number 99610 (in bold) are listed as follows:

Table 4.37 Corresponding rule and standard score of chunks with original serial number 83754

Original serial number	Chunk	Chinese translation	Corresponding rule	Standard score
83754	E83754 = shipping advice	C83754a = 装运通知	① E83754 ≈ C83754a	88
		C83754b = 装船通知	② E83754 ≈ C83754b	12

(1) The insurance companies, on knowing this, will shift their responsibilities to the goods being packed in cartons not fit for ocean transportation and refuse compensation for losses.
(保险公司知道这一点，他们将责任转移到纸箱包装不适合的远洋运输而拒绝赔偿。)
(2) The cartons we use are up to standard and fit for **ocean transportation.**
(我们使用的纸箱均达到标准, 适合远洋运输。)
(3) The cartons are then packed in strong wooden crates which are suitable for long distance **ocean transportation.**
(然后纸箱包装用适合于海洋运输的加厚木箱。)

In these example sentences, the original serial number of 99610, the chunk "ocean transportation" appears 3 times in the corpus. It is found that the Chinese translation of the sentences (1) and (2) are "远洋运输", while that of the sentence (3) is "海洋运输". Therefore, they are in incomplete correspondence. Corresponding rule ① is E99610 ≈ C99610a, where E99610 stands for "ocean transportation" and C99610a for "远洋运输"; the corresponding ratio is 67% and the standard score is 67. Corresponding rule ② is E99610 ≈ C99610b, where C99610b stands for "海洋运输"; the corresponding ratio is 33% and the standard score is 33 (see Table 4.38).

The sentences containing the chunk with the original serial number 101838 (in bold) are listed as follows:

(1) **Please see to it that** the goods will reach us as soon as possible.
(请确保货物及时运往我方。)
(2) And in the meantime, **please see to it that** the L/C stipulations are in strict conformity with those of the confirmation to avoid subsequent amendments of discrepancies in the L/C.

Table 4.38 Corresponding rule and standard score of chunks with original serial number 99610

Original serial number	Chunk	Chinese translation	Corresponding rule	Standard score
99610	E99610 = ocean transportation	C99610a = 远洋运输	① E99610 ≈ C99610a	67
		C99610b = 海洋运输	② E99610 ≈ C99610b	33

(同时, 请确保信用证中的条款严格符合确认书中的, 以避免日后修改信用证中的差异。)

(3) In order to avoid subsequently amendments, **please see to it that** the L/C stipulations are in exact accordance with the terms of the sales confirmation.
(为了避免以后的修订, 请确保 L/C 提单的规定和该销售条款完全一致。)

(4) Meanwhile, **please see to it that** the stipulations in the relative credit should strictly conform to the terms in our sales confirmation in order to avoid subsequent amendments.
(同时, 请确保相关信贷规定严格按照我方的销售确认条款以避免日后修改。)

(5) When you do it, you are requested to be careful. **Please see to it that** the L/C stipulations are in full accordance with the terms and conditions of the contract, so that there will not be amendment to the L/C and we can execute the contract within the prescribed date.
(请仔细开证, 确保信用证规定与合同条款完全一致, 以便不用修改信用证就使我们能在规定的日期内履行合同。)

In these example sentences, the original serial number of "please see to it that" is 101838, and its frequency in the corpus is 5. The corresponding translations of sentences (1)–(4) are all "请确保", while that of sentence (5) is "请……确保". Therefore, they are in incomplete correspondence. Corresponding rule ① is E101838 ≈ C101838a, where E101838 stands for "please see to it that" and C101838a for "请确保"; the corresponding ratio is 80% and the standard score is 80. Corresponding rule ② is E101838 ≈ C101838b, where C101838b stands for "请……确保"; the corresponding ratio is 20% and the standard score is 20 (see Table 4.39).

The sentences containing the chunk with the original serial number 104709 (in bold) are listed as follows:

(1) As we thought there might be a sales potential in your market, too, we shall be glad to supply you with our samples as well as the price list. Your **early reply will be highly appreciated**.
(由于我们公司认为这一新产品在贵方市场也具有潜力, 因此特向贵公司提供相关样品和报价。你方若能尽早答复我方将非常感激。)

(2) If you can accept our delivery requirement, we will sign the contract with you this month. Your **early reply will be highly appreciated**.
(如果你们能接受我们的发货要求, 我们将会在这个月与你们签订合同。你方若能尽早答复我方将非常感激。)

Table 4.39 Corresponding rule and standard score of chunks with original serial number 101838

Original serial number	Chunk	Chinese translation	Corresponding rule	Standard score
101838	E101838 = please see to it that	C101838a = 请确保	① E101838 ≈ C101838a	80
		C101838b = 请……确保	② E101838 ≈ C101838b	20

(3) Your kindness in giving priority to the consideration of the above request and giving us an **early reply will be highly appreciated**.
(您若能优先考虑上述要求并给予尽早**答复，**我方将非常**感激**。)

In these example sentences, the original serial number of "early reply will be highly appreciated" is 104709, and its frequency is 3. The corresponding Chinese translations of sentences (1) and (2) are "尽早答复我方将非常感激", while that of sentence (3) is "尽早答复，我方将非常感激", indicating an incomplete correspondence. Corresponding rule ① is E104709 ≈ C104709a, where E104709 stands for "early reply will be highly appreciated" and C104709a for "尽早答复我方将非常感激"; the corresponding ratio is 67%, and the standard score is 67. Corresponding rule ② is E104709 ≈ C104709b, where C104709b stands for "尽早答复，我方将非常感激"; the corresponding ratio is 33% and the standard score is 33 (see Table 4.40).

The sentences containing the chunk with the original serial number 115450 (in bold) are listed as follows:

(1) We are pleased to inform you that we can supply the fancy plastic goods included in your order No. 676 of 7th February and in accordance with our **terms of payment** for overseas buyers enclose our draft at 30 days for acceptance by your bankers.
(根据贵公司 2 月 7 日的第 676 号订单及贵公司提供的海外买方的付款条件，本公司愿意供应贵公司高级塑胶物品，并附上 30 日期限的汇票，由贵公司的代理银行接收。)
(2) In keeping with our usual **terms of payment** we have drawn on you at 60 days and passed the draft and shipping documents to our bankers.
(依照一贯的付款条件，60 天内向贵公司提款，现已将汇票及货运文件送交贵公司的银行。)
(3) Our **terms of payment** is confirmed and irrevocable letter of credit.
(我们的付款条件是保兑的不可撤销的信用证。)
(4) It would also be appreciated if you could tell us the **terms of payment** on which you do business with others. We trust you will give us an early reply.
(恳请告知贵方与其他客户合作的付款条件，期盼贵方早日答复。)
(5) **Terms of payment** have now been agreed.
(付款条件现已得到认可。)

Table 4.40 Corresponding rule and standard score of chunks with original serial number 104709

Original serial number	Chunk	Chinese translation	Corresponding rule	Standard score
104709	E104709 = early reply will be highly appreciated	C104709a = 尽早答复我方将非常感激	① E104709 ≈ C104709a	67
		C104709b = 尽早答复，我方将非常感激	② E104709 ≈ C104709b	33

(6) When replying, please state **terms of payment** and discounts you would allow on purchases of quantities of over 100 dozen of individual items.
(如果回复, 请说明付款条件和允许的对个别项目超过 100 打的购买数量的折扣。)
(7) **Terms of Payment**: By Confirmed Irrevocable L/C to be opened by Buyers.
(付款条件: 用买方开出的保兑、不可撤销信用证。)
(8) We shall appreciate it if you e-mail us your catalogues with details of your prices and **terms of payment**.
(如果能把你方目录、价格细单和付款条件发邮件过来, 我们将不胜感激。)
(9) We agree to accept the **terms of payment** you proposed.
(我们同意你关于付款条件的建议。)
(10) Will you please send me a copy of your glove catalogue, with details of your prices and **terms of payment**?
(能否请你寄来贵公司的手套商品名录一份, 并请附寄有关价目与付款条件?).
(11) Our usual **terms of payment** are one month from date of invoice and we hope they will be satisfactory to you.
(我公司一贯的付款条件是在发票日期后一个月缴清, 希望能令贵公司满意。)
(12) Our usual **terms of payment** are by confirmed, irrevocable letter of credit for the full amount of the invoice value to be established in our favor, available by draft at sight, reaching us one month ahead of shipment, remaining valid for negotiation in China till the 21st day after the prescribed time of shipment, and allowing transshipment and partial shipment.
(我们一贯的付款条件是采用保兑的、不可撤销的、金额为发票的全部数额的、以我方为抬头人的即期信用证, 于装运前一个月寄至我们。信用证在中国的议付有效期为规定的装运期后 21 天止, 且准许转船和分批装运。)
(13) This is the normal **terms of payment** in international business.
(这是国际贸易中惯用的付款方式。)
(14) The **terms of payment** allow the 3% cash discount only on accounts paid within fourteen days of statement, whereas your present is more than a month overdue.
(虽然我公司付款条款规定在收货后 14 天内结账可以减收 3%, 但您的账款逾期 1 个月才缴清。)
(15) It would seem, however, that we misunderstood your **terms of payment** and in the circumstances should grateful if you could allow us to defer payment for a further three weeks.
(然而, 我公司可能误解了贵公司的付款条款, 在此情况下, 恳请容许我公司再延期三周付账。)
(16) We grant the request as an exceptional measure only because of the promptness with which you have settled your accounts in the past and hope that in future dealings you will be able to keep our **terms of payment**.

(我们准予这个要求, 是作为一个特例处理, 因为过去您一直准时结账, 并希望您在将来的交易中能遵守我公司的付款条款。)

In these example sentences, the original serial number of "terms of payment" is 115450, with a frequency of 16. It is found that the Chinese translations of sentences (1)–(12) are "付款条件", those of sentences (14)–(16) are "付款条款", and that of sentence (13) is "付款方式". Therefore, they are in incomplete correspondence. Corresponding rule ① is E115450 ≈ C115450a, where E115450 stands for "terms of payment" and C115450a for "付款条件"; the corresponding ratio is 75% and the standard score is 75. Corresponding rule ② is E115450 ≈ C115450b, where C115450b stands for "付款条款"; the corresponding ratio is 19%, and the standard score is 19. Corresponding rule ③ is E115450 ≈ C115450c, where C115450c stands for "付款方式"; the corresponding ratio is 6%, and the standard score is 6 (see Table 4.41).

The sentences containing the chunk with the original serial number 115471 (in bold) are listed as follows:

(1) We are satisfied with the quality and pleased to enclose our Order No. 86 for sizes mentioned in your **latest catalogue**.
(我们对产品的质量非常满意, 很高兴在您的**最新**目录中附上了我们86 号订单的尺寸。)
(2) We are sending you our quotation sheet and a copy of our **latest catalogue** giving the details you asked for, and hope that some of our products will be suitable for your market.
(我们向您发送了您需要的详细的产品报价表和**最新**目录, 并希望我们的一些产品适合你方市场。)
(3) Enclosed is our **latest catalogue** which we hope will give the details you want.
(随函附上你想要的详细的**最新**产品目录。)
(4) As you may not be familiar with the wide range of our products, we are enclosing a copy of our **latest catalogue**.
(由于贵方可能不太熟悉我方其他更广范围的产品, 随函附上一份我方**最新**目录的副本。)

In these example sentences, the original serial number of "latest catalogue" is 115471, and its frequency in the corpus is 4. The translations of sentences (1), (2)

Table 4.41 Corresponding rule and standard score of chunks with original serial number 115450

Original serial number	Chunk	Chinese translation	Corresponding rule	Standard score
115450	E115450 = terms of payment	C115450a = 付款条件	① E115450 ≈ C115450a	75
		C115450b = 付款条款	② E115450 ≈ C115450b	19
		C115450c = 付款方式	③ E115450 ≈ C115450c	6

and (4) are all “最新目录”, while the that of sentence (3) is “最新……目录”. Therefore, it is an incomplete correspondence. Correspondence rule ① is E115471 ≈ C115471a, where E115471 stands for “latest catalogue” and C115471a for “最新目录”; the corresponding ratio is 75% and the standard score is 75. Corresponding rule ② is E115471 ≈ C115471b, where C115471b stands for “最新……目录”; the corresponding ratio is 25%. and the standard score is 25 (see Table 4.42).

The sentences containing the chunk with the original serial number 128580 (in bold) are listed as follows:

(1) Many reports have been received from our sales agents in Hong Kong, that there are very **brisk demand** for the captioned garments.
(我们已收到许多来自香港销售商的报告, 标题项下的服装有旺盛的需求。)
(2) We shall appreciate it if you will expedite the shipment of our order as soon as possible thus enabling them to catch the **brisk demand** at the start of the season.
(如果您能尽快装运我方所订购货物, 使它们能够在销售季节一开始就赶上旺盛的需求, 我们将不胜感激。)
(3) We would suggest that you send us your trial orders as soon as possible, as there is a **brisk demand** for this article.
(由于这款产品旺盛的需求, 敬请贵方尽早发出试订单。)
(4) As the selling season is rapidly approaching, we shall appreciate it very much if you will book shipping space and arrange shipment as soon as possible, thus enabling the goods to catch the **brisk demand** at the start of the season.
(鉴于销售旺季迅速接近, 如果贵方能够尽快订舱和安排运输, 使这批货物能够在销售季节一开始就赶上旺盛的需求, 我方将不胜感激。)
(5) As you are aware that there has been lately a **brisk demand** for the above commodities, such growing demand has doubtlessly resulted in increased prices.
(如你所知, 最近市场对以上产品的需求旺盛, 不断增长的需求已毫无疑问引起价格的上涨。)

In these example sentences, the original serial number of “brisk demand” is 128580, with a frequency of 5. We find that the translations of sentences (1)–(4) are “旺盛的需求”, while that of sentence (5) is “需求旺盛”. Therefore, they are in incomplete correspondence. Corresponding rule ① is E128580 ≈ C128580a, where E128580 stands for “brisk demand” and C128580a for “旺盛的需求”; the corresponding ratio is 80% and the standard score is 80. Correspondence rule ② is E128580

Table 4.42 Corresponding rule and standard score of chunks with original serial number 115471

Original serial number	Chunk	Chinese translation	Corresponding rule	Standard score
115471	E115471 = latest catalogue	C115471a = 最新目录	① E115471 ≈ C115471a	75
		C115471b = 最新……目录	② E115471 ≈ C115471b	25

Table 4.43 Corresponding rule and standard score of chunks with original serial number 128580

Original serial number	Chunk	Chinese translation	corresponding rule	Standard score
128580	E128580 = brisk demand	C128580a = 旺盛的需求	① E128580 ≈ C128580a	80
		C128580b = 需求旺盛	② E128580 ≈ C128580b	20

≈ C128580b, where C128580b stands for "需求旺盛"; the corresponding ratio is 20% and the standard score is 20 (see Table 4.43).

The sentences containing the chunk with the original serial number 135671 (in bold) are listed as follows:

(1) We also **want to know** how long it will take if you work on this project.
(我们还想了解, 如果将工程交给你们, 需要多长时间完成。)
(2) If you **want to know** more, please call us on 88888.
(如果您想了解更多, 请拨打我们的电话 88888 来获取更多详情。)
(3) Now we **want to know** whether your MAC[10] is still in a good state.
(现在, 我们想了解一下您的计算机是否仍然使用良好。)
(4) We wish to establish business relations with you and here we **want to know** whether it is possible to push the sales of Stainless-steel Washbasins in your market.
(我方希望与贵公司建立业务关系, 同时我方想了解贵方是否有意在你们的市场上推销我们的不锈钢洗脸盆。)
(5) In addition, we still **want to know** your earliest delivery date and discounts for regular purchases.
(另外, 我们还想知道贵公司最早的交货日期及定期购买的折扣。)

In these example sentences, the original serial number of "want to know" is 135671, and its frequency is 5. The translations of the sentences (1)–(4) are "想了解", while that of sentence (5) is "想知道", showing an incomplete correspondence. Corresponding rule ① is E135671 ≈ C135671a, where E135671 stands for "want to know" and C135671a for "想了解"; the corresponding ratio is 80% and the standard score is 80. Corresponding rule ② is E135671 ≈ C135671b, where C135671b stands for "想知道"; the corresponding ratio is 20% and the standard score is 20 (see Table 4.44).

The sentences containing the chunk with the original serial number 140133 (in bold) are listed as follows:

(1) We **thank you for your letter** of 3rd August and are glad you think that a satisfactory market could be found for our goods, but are not altogether happy at the prospect of transacting all our business on a credit basis.
(多谢您 8 月 3 日的来信, 并欣闻贵公司能为我公司产品开发新市场。但对以记账方式交易前景, 不十分满意。)

[10] Multi-access Computer.

Table 4.44 Corresponding rule and standard score of chunks with original serial number 135671

Original serial number	Chunk	Chinese translation	Corresponding rule	Standard score
135671	E135671 = want to know	C135671a = 想了解	① E135671 ≈ C135671a	80
		C135671b = 想知道	② E135671 ≈ C135671b	20

(2) **Thank you for your letter** of 12th May enquiring about the shipment of the captioned goods.
(多谢您 5 月 12 日询问有关标题货物装运情况的来信。)
(3) **Thank you for your letter** of 20th May requesting earlier delivery of goods under your purchase contract No.954.
(多谢您 5 月 20 日有关要求提早装运第 954 号合约的来信。)
(4) **Thank you for your letter** of 24th August enclosing your cheque for 45,000 RMB in full settlement of the amount due on our July settlement.
(多谢您 8 月 24 日的来信及人民币 45 000 元支票一张, 作为缴清 7. 月份账款之用。)
(5) We **thank you for your letter** of 5th July and are pleased to learn that you like our cameras.
(多谢您 7 月 5 日的来信, 得知您喜爱本公司出产的相机, 很是高兴。)
(6) We **thank you for your letter** of yesterday and your cheque for 9,700 RMB, which you sent in full settlement of our August statement.
(多谢您昨天的来信及人民币 9700 元支票一张, 作为缴清 8 月份决算表之用。)
(7) **Thank you for your letter** of 9th May enclosing a cheque for 4,000 RMB in part payment of the balance due on our April statement.
(多谢您 5 月 9 日的来信及附寄的人民币 4000 元整支票一张, 作为缴清 4 月份结算单部分账款。)
(8) Thank you for your letter of 5th July.
(多谢您方 7 月 5 日的来信。)
(9) I write to **thank you for your letter** of 9th October and for the samples of cotton shirt you very kindly sent me.
(多谢您 10 月 9 日的来信及棉布衬衫样品。)
(10) **Thank you for your letter** of 7th April.
(多谢您 4 月 7 日的来信。)
(11) We **thank you for your letter** of 10th September informing us of the wrong delivery of the laser printer.
(多谢您方 9 月 10 日的来信告知激光打印机发错了货。)
(12) **Thank you for your letter** of 20th January.
(多谢您方 1 月 20 日的来信。)
(13) **Thank you for your letter** of 20th May proposing a sole agency for our stain less steel cutlery.
(多谢您方5 月20 日有关建议担任我方不锈钢刀具之独家代理的来信。)

(14) **Thank you for your letter** of February 10th informing us that the consignment was delivered promptly.
(多谢您方二月十日的来信通知我们货物已经及时交付。)

(15) **Thank you for your letter** of 20th May suggesting that we grant you a sole agency for our "Yang Guang" brand household linens.
(多谢您 5 月 20 日有关建议担任"阳光"牌日用织品代理的来信。)

(16) **Thank you for your letter** of August 5th sending us your quotation and samples.
(多谢您 8 月 5 日的来信及寄送的报价单和样品。)

(17) **Thank you for your letter** of the day before reporting the fire in your factory stores.
(多谢您前天的来信, 报告有关贵厂仓库火灾一事。)

(18) **Thank you for your letter** of January 25th and the enclosed sample of silk bathrobe.
(多谢您 1 月 25 号的来信以及随函附上的丝绸浴衣样品。)

(19) We **thank you for your letter** of September 9th, informing us of your client's comments on our packing.
(我们多谢您 9 月 9 日的来信以及告知您的客户对我们的评论。)

(20) **Thank you for your letter** of 18th May.
(多谢您 5 月 18 日的来信。)

(21) **Thank you for your letter** of February 10th informing us that the consignment was delivered promptly.
(多谢您 2 月 10 日的来信通知我们货物及时运抵。)

(22) **Thank you for your letter** of July 15th, inquiring for 100,000 yards printed shirting.
(多谢您 7 月 15 日的来信, 查询 100 000 码印花衬衫面料。)

(23) **Thank you for your letter** of Aug. 19th sending us your quotation and samples.
(多谢您 8 月 19 日寄送给我们的报价单和样品的来信。)

(24) I **thank you for your letter** of 5th July and for your invitation to represent you in this market.
(多谢您 7 月 5 日的来信, 并感谢被您邀请为市场代表。)

(25) We **thank you for your letter** of the day before and are pleased to inform that we will hold this property covered for U.S. $75, 000 as from 24th March on the terms and conditions of the company's comprehensive policy.
(多谢您前天的来信, 并很高兴通知您, 我公司承保上述房产, 保额为 75 000 美元, 保期自 3 月 24 日开始, 一切根据我公司综合保险条款执行。)

(26) **Thank you for your letter** of 10th June sending us patterns of cotton prints.
(多谢您 6 月 10 日的来信, 并寄送给我公司印花棉布的花样。)

(27) **Thank you for your letter** of 24th March forwarding booklet with details of your range of wrist watches.
(多谢您 3 月 24 日的来信, 送来我公司手表的详细小册子。)

(28) We **thank you for your letter** of 25th August and accept with pleasure your proposal to send us a representative selection of your plastics on a consignment basis.

(多谢您 8 月 25 日的来信, 并乐意接受有关寄售贵公司具有代表性的塑胶制品的提议。)

(29) **Thank you for your letter** of 16th February.
(多谢您方 2 月 16 日的来信。)

(30) We **thank you for your letter** dated March 15th, contents of which have been duly noted.
(多谢您 3 月 15 日来信, 我方对此信给予了充分的关注。)

(31) We **thank you for your letter** of May 9th, quoting us for 3, 000 cases of iron nails on CIF terms.
(谢谢您 5 月 9 日的来信, 获悉 3000 箱铁钉按到岸价报价。)

(32) **Thank you for your letter** of 10th February requesting an earlier delivery of goods under your purchase contract No. 953.
(谢谢您 2 月 10 号的来信, 有关要求你方采购合同第 953 号的货物尽早交货。)

(33) **Thank you for your letter** of September 26, offering us Cotton Sweaters.
(谢谢您 9 月 26 日的来信, 向我们提供棉毛衣。)

(34) **Thank you for your letter** and suggestion.
(谢谢你的来信和建议。)

(35) **Thank you for your letter** of April 25th concerning the consumer goods.
(谢谢您 4 月 25 日有关消费品的来信。)

(36) **Thank you for your letter** of March 22, informing us that the subject goods could be shipped.
(谢谢您 3 月 22 日的来信, 通知我们主题货物可以运。)

(37) We **thank you for your letter** of May 10th, and understand your concern with packing.
(我们谢谢您 5 月 10 日的来信, 并理解你方有关包装的事宜。)

(38) **Thank you for your letter** and samples sent on June 15th.
(多谢您的来信以及 6 月 15 日发送的样品。)

(39) **Thank you for your letter** enclosing an account of the organization and work of your local trade association.
(多谢您的来信及附带的当地贸易协会的组织及工作报告。)

(40) **Thank you for your letter** and I'm looking for cooperating with you as soon as possible.
(多谢您的来信, 也期待尽快和您进行合作。)

(41) **Thank you for your letter** but we wish to invite your attention to our order No.6241.
(多谢您的来信, 但我们想请你注意我们的第 6241 号订单。)

(42) **Thank you for your letter** and for your question as well.
(非常感谢您的来信以及你提出的问题。)

(43) **Thank you for your letter** and the catalogues and price lists.
(感谢您的来信以及这些产品目录和价目表。)

In these example sentences, the original serial number of "Thank you for your letter" is 140133, with a frequency of 43 in the corpus. After analyzing the 43 examples, we find that the corresponding translations of sentences (1)–(30) are "多谢

您……的来信", those of the sentences (31)–(37) are "谢谢您……的来信",those of the sentences (38)–(41) are "多谢您的来信", and those of the sentences (42)–(43) are "感谢您的来信". Therefore, they are in incomplete correspondence. Corresponding rule ① is E140133 ≈ C140133a, where E140133 stands for "thank you for your letter" and C140133a for "多谢您……的来信"; the corresponding ratio is 70%, converted to the standard score of 70. Corresponding rule ② is E140133 ≈ C140133b, where C140133b stands for "谢谢您……的来信"; the corresponding ratio is 16%, converted to the standard score 16. Corresponding rule ③ is E140133 ≈ C140133c, where C140133c stands for "多谢您的来信"; the corresponding ratio is 9%, converted to the standard score of 16. Corresponding rule ④ is E140133 ≈ C140133d, where C140133d stands for "感谢您的来信"; the corresponding ratio is 5%, converted to the standard score of 5 (see Table 4.45).

The sentences containing the chunk with the original serial number 146079 (in bold) are listed as follows:

(1) We **find both quality and prices satisfactory**. Enclosed herewith, please find our order No. 363.
(我们对产品质量和价格都非常满意。随函附上订单，请查收 363 号。)
(2) We **find both quality and prices satisfactory**.
(我公司对产品质量和价格都非常满意。)
(3) We **find both quality and prices satisfactory** and are pleased to give you an order for the following items on the understanding that they will be supplied from current stock at the price names.
(我公司对于品质和价格均感满意，更乐意在指定价格及供应现货的条件下订购下列货物。)

In these example sentences, the original serial number of "find both quality and prices satisfactory" is 146079, and its frequency is 3. The Chinese translations of sentences (1) and (2) are "对产品质量和价格都非常满意", while that of sentence (3) is "对于品质和价格均感满意". Therefore, they are in incomplete correspondence. Corresponding rule ① is E146079 ≈ C146079a, where E146079 stands for "find both quality and prices satisfactory" and C146079a for "对产品质量和价格

Table 4.45 Corresponding rule and standard score of chunks with original serial number 140133

Original serial number	Chunk	Chinese translation	Corresponding rule	Standard score
140133	E140133 = thank you for your letter	C140133a = 多谢您……的来信	① E140133 ≈ C140133a	70
		C140133b = 谢谢您……的来信	② E140133 ≈ C140133b	16
		C140133c = 多谢您的来信	③ E140133 ≈ C140133c	9
		C140133d = 感谢您的来信	④ E140133 ≈ C140133d	5

都非常满意";the corresponding ratio of 67% and the standard score is 67. Corresponding rule ② is E146079 ≈ C146079b, where C146079b stands for "对于品质和价格均感满意", with a corresponding rate of 33% and a standard score of 33 (see Table 4.46).

The sentences containing the chunk with the original serial number 149386 (in bold) are listed as follows:

(1) We are sorry you find it necessary to **make this request**, especially at this late stage.
(我公司对您在最后阶段提出这个要求, 深感遗憾。)
(2) As you are aware, my accounts with you have always been settled promptly and it is with utmost regret that I am now forced to **make this request**.
(您知道, 本公司一向按时结账, 现在迫不得已提出这个要求。)
(3) I am sorry to **make this request** so late, but hope that, because of our long-standing business connection, you will see your way to agree.
(我很抱歉这么迟才提出这个要求, 但希望看在我们长久以来业务往来的份上, 请您允许这个要求。)
(4) I **make this request**, I feel that not enough weight could have been given to the following conditions when the present rate of premium was fixed.
(本人提出这个要求, 是由于感到在目前保率确定之前, 未曾考虑下列情况。)
(5) We are very much regret to **make this request**, but hope you will be able to grant it.
(非常抱歉提出此要求, 望您准许。)

In these example sentences, the original serial number of "make this request" is 149386, with a frequency of 5. The Chinese translations of sentences (1)–(4) are "提出这个要求", while that of sentence (5) is "提出此要求". Therefore, they are incomplete correspondence. Corresponding rule ① is E149386 ≈ C149386a, where E149386 stands for "make this request" and C149386a for "提出这个要求"; the corresponding ratio is 80% and the standard score is 80. Corresponding rule ② is E149386 ≈ C149386b, where C149386b stands for "提出此要求"; the corresponding ratio is 20% and the standard score is 20 (see Table 4.47).

The sentences containing the chunk with the original serial number 152019 (in bold) are listed as follows:

Table 4.46 Corresponding rule and standard score of chunks with original serial number 146079

Original serial number	Chunk	Chinese translation	Corresponding rule	Standard score
146079	E146079 = find both quality and prices satisfactory	C146079a = 对产品质量和价格都非常满意	① E146079 ≈ C146079a	67
		C146079b = 对于品质和价格均感满意	② E146079 ≈ C146079b	33

Table 4.47 Corresponding rule and standard score of chunks with original serial number 149386

Original serial number	Chunk	Chinese translation	Corresponding rule	Standard score
149386	E149386 = make this request	C149386a = 提出这个要求	① E149386 ≈ C149386a	80
		C149386b = 提出此要求	② E149386 ≈ C149386b	20

(1) We find your suggested terms satisfactory and shall be glad to receive your **formal agreement** for signature.
(我公司觉得贵公司所提条件合理, 并乐意签署正式合约。)
(2) We set our below the terms discussed and agreed with Mr. Horton when he called here earlier this month, but before drafting the **formal agreement** we should like you to confirm them.
(本月前些时间贵公司的何顿先生到访, 曾商讨并同意我公司所定以下条款, 但在未起草正式合约前, 我还望您核实以下各项。)
(3) I shall be glad if you will kindly confirm these terms. I will then arrange for a **formal agreement** to be drafted and copies sent for your signature.
(希望您证实同意以上条款, 然后由我方起草正式合约, 再寄副本给您签署。)
(4) If you will confirm these terms we will arrange for a **formal agreement** to be drawn up and, when this is signed, prepare a circular for distribution to our customers in Ireland announcing your appointment as our agents.
(若贵公司接受上述条件, 本公司将安排签署正式合约。签约完毕, 将通知分发给本公司在爱尔兰地区的客户, 宣布委任您为代理人。)
(5) If security is deposited we shall be willing to protect your interests by entering into a **formal agreement** giving you the sole agency for a period of five years.
(在保证金存妥后, 本公司愿意与您签署正式合约, 并给予为期五年的独家代理权, 以保障您的利益。)
(6) If you are interested in our proposal, we suggest a **formal agreement** on the lines of model agreement enclosed.
(如有意的话, 我们建议签署一项正式协议。另附上样本细则一份。)

In these example sentences, the original serial number of "formal agreement" is 152019, with a frequency of 6. The Chinese translations of sentences (1)–(5) are "正式合约", while that of sentence (6) is "正式协议", indicating an incomplete correspondence. Corresponding rule ① is E152019 ≈ C152019a, where E152019 stands for "formal agreement" and C152019a for "正式合约"; the corresponding ratio is 83% and the standard score is 83. Corresponding rule ② is E152019 ≈ C152019b, where C152019b stands for "正式协议"; the corresponding ratio is 17% and the standard score is 17 (see Table 4.48).

Through analysis above, we have summarized the following rules:

First, the differences in translation are caused by the translator's arbitrariness. For example, the translations in the corpus of "special discount" are "特别折扣"

Table 4.48 Corresponding rule and standard score of chunks with original serial number 152019

Original serial number	Chunk	Chinese translation	Corresponding rule	Standard score
152019	E152019 = formal agreement	C152019a = 正式合约	① E152019 ≈ C152019a	83
		C152019b = 正式协议	② E152019 ≈ C152019b	17

and "特殊折扣", which do not have substantial discrepancy in meaning. According to the Chinese dictionary, "特殊" refers to fewer amounts, such as "特殊照顾" (special care) and "特殊保护" (special protection). However, "特别" refers to more amounts, such as "特别喜欢" (like somebody or something particularly) and "特别想念" (miss somebody or something very much). Moreover, the word "特别" also means "especially/extra". In the context of this chapter, "special discount" means an additional discount given by the seller when the purchase meet the seller's requirements, which is objective and applies to any customer who cuts the mustard, whereas "特殊" is characterized by emotion and arbitrariness. Therefore, "特别折扣" is more appropriate here, consistent with the situation presented in the corpus. Meanwhile, the author searched the Texts of Recent Chinese (Online Edition) (URL: http://ccl.pku.edu.cn:8080/ccl_corpus/index.jsp?dir=xiandai) of the Center for Chinese Linguistics of Peking University for these two expressions. It shows that there are three examples containing "特别折扣" while no results for "特殊折扣". In this case, the author believes that the translator's choice of words should be standardized by means of a dictionary or others. The same goes for "感谢", "多谢" and "谢谢" (different translations of "Thank you"). It is undeniable that they also involve stylistic factors, which are not discussed in this chapter due to the limited space.

Second, Chinese and English expression habits lead to different translations. For example, "provide a guarantor" are translated into "提供担保人" and "提供……担保人". However, if we take the original text into consideration, the former is "provide a guarantor" while the latter is "provide a guarantor acceptable to us". As we know, adjectival phrases postposed as an attribute is common in English. But when translated into Chinese, the attribute is usually placed before the noun, forming a "adjective + noun" pattern, which naturally separates the verb from the noun object, thus making "verb + noun" become "verb + adjective + noun". Obviously, this difference is superficial, mainly stemming from the fundamental difference between English and Chinese languages in terms of word order.

Third, the differences are caused by the simplification of the translation language. For instance, most translations of "find both quality and prices satisfactory" are "对产品质量和价格都非常满意", while the rest is "对于品质和价格均感满意". As for the latter version, the translator deletes the sentence mainly based on the paratactic syntax and simplicity of Chinese. Similarly, in the translation of "make this request", there are two kinds of translations, namely, "提出这个要求" and "提出此要求", and the latter is also a reflection of the translator's pursuit of simplicity.

C. Zero correspondence and its corresponding rules

It is found that "pleased to inform" and its translations are in zero correspondence. Here is its correspondence relationship, corresponding rules and standard scores.

The sentences containing the chunk with the original serial number 29315 (in bold) are listed as follows:

(1) We are **pleased to inform** you that your transaction has been completed and your order has been shipped.
(很高兴通知您, 您的交易已经完成, 订单也已经出货了。)
(2) We are **pleased to inform** you that we have recently brought out a new product the Automatic Punch.
(很高兴通知贵公司我们最近推出了一种新型的自动打孔机。)
(3) We are so **pleased to inform** you that we offer maintenance service in Hong Kong from now on.
(很高兴通知贵用户, 自即日起, 本公司将在香港地区提供维修服务。)
(4) We are so **pleased to inform** you that our products have been increasingly diverse and our service has been greatly improved this year, which will surely surprise you.
(很高兴通知您, 今年我们的产品种类繁多, 我们的服务也获得了很大的改善。相信它们一定会让您感到惊讶。)
(5) We are **pleased to inform** you that we are one of the leading manufacturers of electric appliance in this city with a history of over 75 years.
(我们很高兴通知您, 我们是这个城市领先的电器制造商之一, 有超过 75 年的历史。)
(6) I'm **pleased to inform** you that your application has been accepted.
(我很高兴通知您, 您的申请已被接受。)
(7) We are **pleased to inform** you that we have booked your order No. 363A for our bikes.
(我们很高兴通知贵方, 我方已收到你们对我们 363 号 A 型自行车的订单。)
(8) Thank you for your order No. 789. We are **pleased to inform** you that we can supply the goods you required, which will be dispatched to you via Hong Kong.
(感谢贵方第 789 号订单。很高兴通知您, 我们能够提供贵方需要的货物, 此批货物将由香港转运。)
(9) We are **pleased to inform** you that the shipment will reach you in time.
(我们很高兴通知您货物将及时抵达。)
(10) We thank you for your letter of the day before and are **pleased to inform** that we will hold this property covered for U.S. $75, 000 as from 24th March on the terms and conditions of the company's comprehensive policy.
(多谢您前天的来信, 并很高兴通知您, 我公司承保上述房产, 保额为 75 000 美元, 保期自 3 月 24 日开始, 一切根据我公司综合保险条款执行。)
(11) However, we are now **pleased to inform** you that we have shipped the mentioned goods on board S.S. Pand which was sailed for your port yesterday directly.

(但是, 该货已于昨日装运上潘迪号轮船, 直接驶往伦敦。) (零翻译、无对应).

(12) We are **pleased to inform** you that we can supply the fancy plastic goods included in your order No. 676 of 7th February and in accordance with our terms of payment for overseas buyers enclose our draft at 30 days for acceptance by your bankers.
(根据贵公司 2 月 7 日的第 676 号订单及贵公司提供的海外买方的付. 款条件, 本公司愿意供应贵公司高级塑胶物品, 并附上 30 日期限的汇票, 由贵公司的代理银行接收。) (零翻译、无对应).

(13) We are **pleased to inform** you that all the goods ordered on the indent enclosed with your letter of 5th July have now been shipped by S.S. Lucky Prince, which sailed from London yesterday and is due to arrive at Alexandria on 8th September.
(贵公司来信及附寄订单上说明的货物, 已经由 "幸运王子"号货轮运载, 该轮昨日离开伦敦, 并将于 9 月 8 日抵达亚历山大港。) (零翻译、无对应).

(14) We are **pleased to inform** you that arrangements have now been made to ship the dress goods you ordered on 14th May.
(您 5 月 14 日所订的衣服已经安排妥当, 准备运出。) (零翻译、无对应).

In these example sentences, the original serial number of "pleased to inform" is 29315, with a frequency of 14 in the corpus. It is found that the Chinese translations of sentences (1)–(10) are "很高兴通知", while sentences (11)–(14) are not translated into the target language, showing a zero correspondence. Corresponding rule ① is E29315 ≈ C29315a, where E29315 stands for "pleased to inform" and C29315a for "很高兴通知", with the corresponding ratio of 71% and the standard score of 71. Corresponding rule ② is E29315*C29315b, where C29315b stands for "zero translation, no correspondence"; the corresponding ratio is 29%, and the standard score is 29 (see Table 4.49).

Zero translation is a common phenomenon in translation practice. Generally, it has two meanings. On the one hand, it refers to deliberately leaving the expressions in the source language untranslated; on the other hand, it means translating without using the existing expressions in the target language. Lefevere (1992) argues that zero translation is the removal of a certain content from the original text. This kind of deletion usually refers to the removal of words that do not conform to the thinking

Table 4.49 Corresponding rule and standard score of chunks with original serial number 29315

Original serial number	Chunk	Chinese translation	Corresponding rule	Standard score
29315	E29315 = pleased to inform	C29315a = 很高兴通知	① E29315 ≈ C29315a	71
		C29315b = "零翻译、无对应"	② E29315*C29315b	29

modes, language habits, expressions of the target language, or unnecessary words in the opinion of the translator, avoiding the cumbersome translation, and making the translation more rigorous, concise and clear, which also causes the phenomenon of zero correspondence in translation. There are some polite words which seem to be meaningless in Chinese. However, it is better not to delete them at will because they imply friendly emotion and attitude, as in the above example:

Original text: We are pleased to inform you that arrangements have now been made to ship the dress goods you ordered on 14th May.

Obviously, "We are pleased to inform you" is omitted, which is stiff and uninspiring, and is not conducive to communication and interpersonal interaction. Therefore, based on the corpus, most translations choose to convey the information of the original text faithfully.

4.4 Table of Corresponding Chunks in English-Chinese Business Correspondences

On the basis of elaborate analysis, a final table of MT-oriented corresponding chunks in English-Chinese business letters is set, as shown in Table 4.50.

Through the statistics of the correspondence block table of English-Chinese business letters for machine translation, the distribution of complete correspondence, incomplete correspondence and zero correspondence is obtained in this chapter, as shown in Table 4.51.

For better visualization, the author creates a diagram as shown in Fig. 4.2.

According to Table 4.51 and Fig. 4.2, there are 227 chunks in complete correspondence, accounting for 92.65%, which can be said to be the majority; while there are 17 chunks in incomplete correspondence, accounting for 6.94% (15 of them are "one-to-two" cases, that is, one MT-oriented chunk in business English letters corresponds to two translations, so that the MT system can match them in terms of the standard score, then supplemented by manual proofreading). Only one chunk is in zero correspondence, accounting for 0.41%, which can be seen as exceptional.

In the table, the majority is in complete correspondence, while is conducive to the MT of English-Chinese business letters, further improving the accuracy of translations.

4.5 Summary

In this chapter, we analyze corresponding relationship between MT-oriented chunks in business English letter and the corresponding translations, set down corresponding rules and standard scores, and develop the table of the MT-oriented corresponding chunks in English-Chinese business letters. In the table, the majority chunks is

Table 4.50 Table of MT-oriented corresponding chunks in English-Chinese business correspondences

No.	Original serial number	Chunk	Chinese translation	Corresponding rule	Standard score
1	2529	E2529 = lead to further business between us	C2529 = 促使我们之间的进一步合作	E2529 = C2529	100
2	2582	E2582 = certainly do our best to make it so	C2582 = 当尽力使之成为事实	E2582 = C2582	100
3	3827	E3827 = dear sir or madam	C3827 = 敬启者	E3827 = C3827	100
4	4301	E4301 = allow you a discount	C4301 = 给予折扣	E4301 = C4301	100
5	4798	E4798 = working relationship	C4798 = 工作关系	E4798 = C4798	100
6	5123	E5123 = contract to be drawn up	C5123 = 拟定合同	E5123 = C5123	100
7	6003	E6003 = pleased to enclose our order no.	C6003 = 高兴地附上我们的订单	E6003 = C6003	100
8	8287	E8287 = quite willing to undertake the training	C8287 = 很愿意接受培训	E8287 = C8287	100
9	9986	E9986 = present salary	C9986 = 现在的薪金	E9986 = C9986	100
10	10007	E10007 = only reason	C10007 = 唯一理由	E10007 = C10007	100
11	10893	E10893 = a sole agency for marketing	C10893 = 市场的独家代理	E10893 = C10893	100
12	13310	E13310 = serve you well	C13310 = 提供良好的服务	E13310 = C13310	100
13	14440	E14440 = past four years	C14440 = 过去四年	E14440 = C14440	100
14	16721	E16721 = representative selection	C16721 = 具有代表性	E16721 = C16721	100
15	17093	E17093 = at an early date	C17093 = 早日	E17093 = C17093	100
16	17510	E17510 = a wide range of	C17510 = 大范围的	E17510 = C17510	100

(continued)

Table 4.50 (continued)

No.	Original serial number	Chunk	Chinese translation	Corresponding rule	Standard score
17	17522	E17522 = many thanks for your quotation	C17522 = 非常感谢您的报价	E17522 = C17522	100
18	17529	E17529 = be glad to learn	C17529 = 欣悉	E17529 = C17529	100
19	20567	E20567 = make clear beforehand	C20567 = 事先明确	E20567 = C20567	100
20	20775	E20775 = packed in international standard	C20775 = 按国际标准包装	E20775 = C20775	100
21	21108	E21108 = which the port of destination and our order number	C21108 = 其……目的港和订单号码	E21108 = C21108	100
22	21662	E21662 = reach you in good time	C21662 = 及时送到贵公司	E21662 = C21662	100
23	22537	E22537 = early decision	C22537 = 尽早决定	E22537 = C22537	100
24	22689	E22689 = local conditions	C22689 = 当地情况	E22689 = C22689	100
25	23485	E23485 = regret to tell you	C23485 = 遗憾地告诉您	E23485 = C23485	100
26	23504	E23504 = goods are shipped	C23504 = 货物运输	E23504 = C23504	100
27	23687	E23687 = no available space	C23687 = 没有剩余货位	E23687 = C23687	100
28	24065	E24065 = an early reply will be obliged	C24065 = 希望能早日得到您的回复	E24065 = C24065	100
29	24782	E24782 = prompt reply will be greatly appreciated	C24782 = 及时回复将非常感谢	E24782 = C24782	100
30	25398	E25398 = be willing to establish business relations with us	C25398 = 愿意与我们建立业务关系	E25398 = C25398	100
31	27018	E27018 = defer payment for a further three weeks	C27018 = 再延期三周付账	E27018 = C27018	100

(continued)

Table 4.50 (continued)

No.	Original serial number	Chunk	Chinese translation	Corresponding rule	Standard score
32	27160	E27160 = defer payment	C27160 = 延期付款	E27160 = C27160	100
33	28885	E28885 = cash discount	C28885 = 现金折扣	E28885 = C28885	100
34	28936	E28936 = in full settlement	C28936 = 缴清	E28936 = C28936	100
35	29315	E29315 = pleased to inform	C29315a = 很高兴通知	① E29315 ≈ C29315a	71
			C29315b="零翻译、无对应"	② E29315* C29315b	29
36	30780	E30780 = payment of the balance	C30780 = 付清余款	E30780 = C30780	100
37	32170	E32170 = good enough	C32170 = 最好	E32170 = C32170	100
38	33751	E33751 = until the end of this year	C33751 = 到年底为止	E33751 = C33751	100
39	35160	E35160 = apply for an overdraft	C35160 = 申请透支	E35160 = C35160	100
40	36586	E36586 = both surprised and disappointed	C36586 = 既惊讶又失望	E36586 = C36586	100
41	37516	E37516 = a trial period of twelve months	C37516 = 试用期为 12 个月	E37516 = C37516	100
42	38557	E38557 = entirely satisfactory	C38557 = 令人满意	E38557 = C38557	100
43	40791	E40791 = date of invoice	C40791 = 发票日期	E40791 = C40791	100
44	40917	E40917 = these prices include packing and delivery	C40917 = 上述价格包括包装费和运费	E40917 = C40917	100
45	41881	E41881 = small profit	C41881 = 薄利	E41881 = C41881	100
46	42198	E42198 = welcome the opportunity to do business with you	C42198 = 希望有机会同你们合作	E42198 = C42198	100

(continued)

Table 4.50 (continued)

No.	Original serial number	Chunk	Chinese translation	Corresponding rule	Standard score
47	42463	E42463 = special discount	C42463a = 特别折扣	① E42463 ≈ C42463a	75
			C42463b = 特殊折扣	② E42463 ≈ C42463b	25
48	42553	E42553 = prices we quoted	C42553 = 我们的报价	E42553 = C42553	100
49	42649	E42649 = sorry to learn from your letter	C42649 = 遗憾地从您的信中得知	E42649 = C42649	100
50	43711	E43711 = forced to cut our prices to the minimum	C43711 = 被迫将定价降至最低	E43711 = C43711	100
51	43795	E43795 = having carefully considered	C43795 = 经慎重考虑	E43795 = C43795	100
52	44317	E41881 = feel confident	C44317 = 自信	E44317 = C44317	100
53	44950	E44950 = find a ready sale	C44950 = 畅销	E44950 = C44950	100
54	45163	E45163 = a ready sale for our products in your market	C45163 = 我们的产品在您方市场上很畅销	E45163 = C45163	100
55	45260	E45260 = an exceptional case	C45260 = 特殊情况	E45260 = C45260	100
56	45418	E45418 = convince you of the reasonableness of our quotation	C45418 = 说服您相信我们报价的合理性	E45418 = C45418	100
57	45512	E45512 = a fair comparison of quality	C45512 = 质量公平的比较	E45512 = C45512	100
58	46104	E46104 = interested in our proposal	C46104 = 对我们的建议感兴趣	E46104 = C46104	100
59	46811	E46811 = provide a guarantor	C46811a = 提供担保人	① E46811 ≈ C46811a	67
			C46811b = 提供……担保人	② E46811 ≈ C46811b	33

(continued)

Table 4.50 (continued)

No.	Original serial number	Chunk	Chinese translation	Corresponding rule	Standard score
60	47560	E47560 = on going into the matter	C47560 = 经调查此事	E47560 = C47560	100
61	47600	E47600 = right goods to be dispatched	C47600 = 发送正确货物	E47600 = C47600	100
62	47611	E47611 = dispatched to you at once	C47611 = 立即发送	E47611 = C47611	100
63	47614	E47614 = relative documents will be mailed	C47614 = 相关文件将邮寄	E47614 = C47614	100
64	48722	E48722 = look forward to receiving your further orders	C48722 = 期望得到贵方更多的订单	E48722 = C48722	100
65	53728	E53728 = due to arrive	C53728 = 预计到达	E53728 = C53728	100
66	55092	E55092 = saving in freight charges	C55092 = 节约运费	E55092 = C55092	100
67	55248	E55248 = the shipping containers we provide	C55248 = 我们提供的集装箱	E55248 = C55248	100
68	55417	E55417 = load and unload at the same time	C55417 = 同时装载和卸载	E55417 = C55417	100
69	56358	E56358 = a thousand tons	C56358 = 上千吨	E56358 = C56358	100
70	57451	E57451 = sent herewith	C57451 = 随函寄上	E57451 = C57451	100
71	57490	E57490 = damaged during transit	C57490 = 运输中受损	E57490 = C57490	100
72	57584	E57584 = regret to note that	C57584 = 遗憾地注意到	E57584 = C57584	100
73	57601	E57601 = clean bill of lading	C57601 = 清洁提单	E57601 = C57601	100

(continued)

Table 4.50 (continued)

No.	Original serial number	Chunk	Chinese translation	Corresponding rule	Standard score
74	57604	E57604 = your claim on order	C57604 = 你方索赔订单	E57604 = C57604	100
75	57658	E57658 = claim to be lodged	C57658 = 提出索赔	E57658 = C57658	100
76	57716	E57716 = suggest you set out a claim immediately	C57716 = 建议你立即提出索赔	E57716 = C57716	100
77	57722	E57722 = hope our explanation will be satisfactory	C57722 = 希望我们的解释将是令人满意的	E57722 = C57722	100
78	57732	E57732 = a claim immediately against the shipping company	C57732 = 立即向装运公司提出索赔	E57732 = C57732	100
79	57754	E57754 = have received your letter of april	C57754 = 已收到你 4 月的来信	E57754 = C57754	100
80	57781	E57781 = good condition when they left here	C57781 = 离开时产品状况良好	E57781 = C57781	100
81	57893	E57893 = goods in question were carefully packed by experienced workmen	C57893 = 商品是由经验丰富的工人经过仔细 包装的	E57893 = C57893	100
82	58084	E58084 = unpacking the cases	C58084 = 打开包装	E58084 = C58084	100
83	58094	E58094 = requirements of this market	C58094 = 市场的要求	E58094 = C58094	100
84	58194	E58194 = must return the goods to you	C58194 = 必须退还你方货物	E58194 = C58194	100
85	58199	E58199 = look forward to your early settlement	C58199 = 期待着您早日结算	E58199 = C58199	100

(continued)

Table 4.50 (continued)

No.	Original serial number	Chunk	Chinese translation	Corresponding rule	Standard score
86	58232	E58232 = found that the quality was not satisfactory	C58232 = 发现质量并不令人满意	E58232 = C58232	100
87	58246	E58246 = for the invoice value and inspection charges involved	C58246 = 所涉及的发票金额和检验费用	E58246 = C58246	100
88	58254	E58254 = regret to inform you	C58254 = 很遗憾地通知您	E58254 = C58254	100
89	58258	E58258 = the survey report issued by beijing commodity inspection bureau	C58258 = 北京商品检验局的质检报告	E58258 = C58258	100
90	58296	E58296 = not up to the standard of samples	C58296 = 达不到标准样品质量	E58296 = C58296	100
91	58298	E58298 = the goods delivered is not up to the standard	C58298 = 交付的货物不符合标准	E58298 = C58298	100
92	58328	E58328 = too inferior to be suitable for the requirements	C58328 = 质量太差而不能符合要求	E58328 = C58328	100
93	58427	E58427 = prepared to consider	C58427 = 准备考虑	E58427 = C58427	100
94	58930	E58930 = shipping documents	C58930a = 货运文件	① E58930 ≈ C58930a	70
			C58930b = 货运单据	② E58930 ≈ C58930b	30
95	58999	E58999 = completely different articles	C58999 = 完全不同的货物	E58999 = C58999	100
96	59930	E59930 = regular customers	C59930 = 老客户	E59930 = C59930	100
97	60086	E60086 = comply with your request	C60086 = 按照你方要求	E60086 = C60086	100
98	60262	E60262 = have no choice but to do so	C60262 = 除此之外别无选择	E60262 = C60262	100

(continued)

Table 4.50 (continued)

No.	Original serial number	Chunk	Chinese translation	Corresponding rule	Standard score
99	61052	E61052 = through a confusion of number	C61052 = 由于数目混淆	E61052 = C61052	100
100	61193	E61193 = did not contain the goods you ordered	C61193 = 不包含你们所订购的货物	E61193 = C61193	100
101	61227	E61227 = a mistake is indeed made in the packing	C61227 = 包装上确实犯了个错误	E61227 = C61227	100
102	61364	E61364 = dress materials supplied	C61364 = 供应的服装材料	E61364 = C61364	100
103	61400	E61400 = after careful examination	C61400 = 经过仔细检查	E61400 = C61400	100
104	61511	E61511 = duly received the documents	C61511 = 如期收到了文件	E61511 = C61511	100
105	62195	E62195 = sincere apologies	C62195 = 深表歉意	E62195 = C62195	100
106	63651	E63651 = kindly requested	C63651 = 谨请	E63651 = C63651	100
107	64061	E64061 = settle the problem	C64061 = 解决问题	E64061 = C64061	100
108	65279	E65279 = many thanks for your letter	C65279 = 非常感谢您的来函	E65279 = C65279	100
109	66000	E66000 = please let me know	C66000a = 请告知我	① E66000 ≈ C66000a	75
			C66000b = 请……告知我	② E66000 ≈ C66000b	25
110	67951	E67951 = reduction in your price	C67951 = 降低价格	E67951 = C67951	100
111	68030	E68030 = enclosed herewith	C68030 = 随函附上	E68030 = C68030	100
112	68443	E68443 = draw your attention	C68443 = 提醒贵方注意	E68443 = C68443	100
113	68762	E68762 = price lists	C68762 = 价目表	E68762 = C68762	100

(continued)

Table 4.50 (continued)

No.	Original serial number	Chunk	Chinese translation	Corresponding rule	Standard score
114	68799	E68799 = various types	C68799 = 各种类型	E68799 = C68799	100
115	68930	E68930 = above will be acceptable to you	C68930 = 以上你会接受	E68930 = C68930	100
116	69685	E69685 = last year	C69685 = 去年	E69685 = C69685	100
117	71210	E71210 = last week	C71210 = 上周	E71210 = C71210	100
118	71950	E71950 = transaction prove to be successful	C71950 = 交易被证明是成功的	E71950 = C71950	100
119	72467	E72467 = in urgent need of these goods	C72467 = 对这些产品的迫切需求	E72467 = C72467	100
120	72496	E72496 = make delivery at an early date	C72496 = 早日交货	E72496 = C72496	100
121	73625	E73625 = please send us your proforma invoice in triplicate	C73625 = 请寄给我们一式三份的形式发票	E73625 = C73625	100
122	73731	E73731 = within the contracted time	C73731 = 在合同规定期内	E73731 = C73731	100
123	74102	E74102 = the delivery date is approaching	C74102 = 交货日期临近	E74102 = C74102	100
124	74449	E74449 = above mentioned	C74449 = 上述	E74449 = C74449	100
125	77261	E77261 = two years ago	C77261 = 两年前	E77261 = C77261	100
126	77426	E77426 = the said license is approved	C77426a = 该许可获得批准	① E77426 ≈ C77426a	67
			C77426b = 上述许可获得批准	② E77426 ≈ C77426b	33
127	78045	E78045 = in this particular line of business	C78045 = 此项业务	E78045 = C78045	100

(continued)

Table 4.50 (continued)

No.	Original serial number	Chunk	Chinese translation	Corresponding rule	Standard score
128	80714	E80714 = enter into business	C80714 = 开始经商	E80714 = C80714	100
129	80835	E80835 = one of the leading importers	C80835 = 主要的进口商之一	E80835 = C80835	100
130	81040	E81040 = mutually beneficial	C81040 = 互惠互利	E81040 = C81040	100
131	81998	E81998 = many years experience in this particular line of business	C81998 = 在此行业已有多年经验	E81998 = C81998	100
132	83754	E83754 = shipping advice	C83754a = 装运通知	① E83754 ≈ C83754a	88
			C83754b = 装船通知	② E83754 ≈ C83754b	12
133	83798	E83798 = due to sail	C83798 = 预计发船期	E83798 = C83798	100
134	83853	E83853 = end of this month	C83853 = 本月底	E83853 = C83853	100
135	84635	E84635 = meet with your approval	C84635 = 得到您的同意	E84635 = C84635	100
136	88255	E88255 = look forward to your early reply	C88255 = 期待着你的早日回复	E88255 = C88255	100
137	88805	E88805 = our offer remains valid for one month	C88805 = 我方报盘保持有效一个月	E88805 = C88805	100
138	88878	E88878 = under separate interest	C88878 = 在另函中	E88878 = C88878	100
139	88933	E88933 = with keen interest	C88933 = 殷切期待	E88933 = C88933	100
140	89250	E89250 = per hundred	C89250 = 每百件	E89250 = C89250	100
141	89293	E89293 = from date of invoice	C89293 = 自发票开出之日起	E89293 = C89293	100

(continued)

Table 4.50 (continued)

No.	Original serial number	Chunk	Chinese translation	Corresponding rule	Standard score
142	90087	E90087 = indeed sorry that you found our price too high	C90087 = 真是遗憾您觉得我们的价格太高	E90087 = C90087	100
143	90147	E90147 = place regular and substantial orders	C90147 = 长期大量订货	E90147 = C90147	100
144	90177	E90177 = have quoted such low prices	C90177 = 报出这样低的价格	E90177 = C90177	100
145	90610	E90610 = to place a trial order	C90610 = 试订	E90610 = C90610	100
146	90653	E90653 = hope you will reconsider	C90653 = 希望你能重新考虑	E90653 = C90653	100
147	90695	E90695 = accept your quotation would mean little profit	C90695 = 接受你的报价将意味着几乎没有利润	E90695 = C90695	100
148	90756	E90756 = all the terms contained in the offer are acceptable	C90756 = 你方报盘中所有条款均可接受	E90756 = C90756	100
149	90769	E90769 = contained in the offer are acceptable except the price	C90769 = 除了价格都是可以接受的	E90769 = C90769	100
150	90771	E90771 = hope you will reconsider this matter	C90771 = 希望您能重新考虑此事	E90771 = C90771	100
151	90835	E90835 = place more substantial orders on a regular basis	C90835 = 更大量的定期订单	E90835 = C90835	100
152	91051	E91051 = must stress	C91051 = 必须强调	E91051 = C91051	100
153	91298	E91298 = push the sales of	C91298 = 推销	E91298 = C91298	100
154	91311	E91311 = quantity discount	C91311 = 数量折扣	E91311 = C91311	100

(continued)

Table 4.50 (continued)

No.	Original serial number	Chunk	Chinese translation	Corresponding rule	Standard score
155	91356	E91356 = thank you for your inquiry	C91356 = 感谢您的询盘	E91356 = C91356	100
156	93385	E93385 = lower than	C93385 = 低于	E93385 = C93385	100
157	95401	E95401 = in wooden cases	C95401 = 木箱包装	E95401 = C95401	100
158	95582	E95582 = packed in cartons	C95582 = 纸箱包装	E95582 = C95582	100
159	96055	E96055 = do not hesitate to let us know	C96055 = 毫不犹豫地告诉我们	E96055 = C96055	100
160	96467	E96467 = mutual benefit	C96467 = 共同利益	E96467 = C96467	100
161	97377	E97377 = keep dry	C97377 = 保持干燥	E97377 = C97377	100
162	97450	E97450 = order number should be stenciled	C97450 = 订单号应该是钢印的	E97450 = C97450	100
163	98959	E98959 = warning marks	C98959 = 警示标志	E98959 = C98959	100
164	99196	E99196 = be packed in international standard tea	C99196 = 符合国际标准的茶盒包装	E99196 = C99196	100
165	99455	E99455 = on the outer packing please mark our initials	C99455 = 请在外包装上注明我方的首字母	E99455 = C99455	100
166	99610	E99610 = ocean transportation	C99610a = 远洋运输	① E99610 ≈ C99610a	67
			C99610b = 海洋运输	② E99610 ≈ C99610b	33
167	100362	E100362 = thank you in advance for your cooperation	C100362 = 预先感谢您的合作	E100362 = C100362	100
168	101838	E101838 = please see to it that	C101838a = 请确保	① E101838 ≈ C101838a	80
			C101838b = 请……确保	② E101838 ≈ C101838b	20

(continued)

Table 4.50 (continued)

No.	Original serial number	Chunk	Chinese translation	Corresponding rule	Standard score
169	101893	E101893 = avoid subsequent amendments	C101893 = 避免日后修改	E101893 = C101893	100
170	102340	E102340 = hope to hear favorably from you	C102340 = 希望听到您满意的答复	E102340 = C102340	100
171	102522	E102522 = time of shipment	C102522 = 装运时间	E102522 = C102522	100
172	102608	E102608 = usual terms of payment	C102608 = 一贯的付款条件	E102608 = C102608	100
173	102695	E102695 = by draft at sight	C102695 = 凭即期汇票支付	E102695 = C102695	100
174	102894	E102894 = look forward to the pleasure of your order	C102894 = 期待着您的订单	E102894 = C102894	100
175	103797	E103797 = date and place of expiry	C103797 = 截止日期和地点	E103797 = C103797	100
176	104190	E104190 = so that we can	C104190 = 以便我们	E104190 = C104190	100
177	104709	E104709 = early reply will be highly appreciated	C104709a = 尽早答复我方将非常感激	① E104709 ≈ C104709a	67
			C104709b = 尽早答复，我方将非常感激	② E104709 ≈ C104709b	33
178	105009	E105009 = favorable reply	C105009 = 有利的答复	E105009 = C105009	100
179	107015	E107015 = payment by confirmed and irrevocable letter of credit	C107015 = 以保兑的不可撤销信用证支付	E107015 = C107015	100
180	111579	E111579 = well aware	C111579 = 当然清楚	E111579 ≈ C111579	100
181	113157	E113157 = other suppliers	C113157 = 其他供应商	E113157 = C113157	100
182	113189	E113189 = quotation sheet	C113189 = 报价单	E113189 = C113189	100

(continued)

Table 4.50 (continued)

No.	Original serial number	Chunk	Chinese translation	Corresponding rule	Standard score
183	113720	E113720 = illustrated catalogues	C113720 = 插图目录	E113720 = C113720	100
184	114413	E114413 = may rest assured	C114413 = 敬请放心	E114413 = C114413	100
185	114797	E114797 = early as possible by direct steamer to hong kong	C114797 = 尽早通过直接的轮船到达香港	E114797 = C114797	100
186	115058	E115058 = not later than	C115058 = 不迟于	E115058 = C115058	100
187	115450	E115450 = terms of payment	C115450a = 付款条件	① E115450 ≈ C115450a	75
			C115450b = 付款条款	② E115450 ≈ C115450b	19
			C115450c = 付款方式	③ E115450 ≈ C115450c	6
188	115471	E115471 = latest catalogue	C115471a = 最新目录	① E115471 ≈ C115471a	75
			C115471b = 最新……目录	② E115471 ≈ C115471b	25
189	115480	E115480 = satisfied with the quality	C115480 = 质量满意	E115480 = C115480	100
190	115506	E115506 = within the next month	C115506 = 在下个月	E115506 = C115506	100
191	116751	E116751 = per dozen	C116751 = 每打	E116751 = C116751	100
192	116774	E116774 = maintain friendly relations	C116774 = 保持友好关系	E116774 = C116774	100
193	117310	E117310 = the wide range of goods we deal in	C117310 = 我方的商品交易范围	E117310 = C117310	100
194	117328	E117328 = enclosing a copy of our catalogue	C117328 = 随函附上一份产品目录	E117328 = C117328	100
195	117358	E117358 = be aware of the wide range of goods	C117358 = 需要了解的各种商品	E117358 = C117358	100

(continued)

Table 4.50 (continued)

No.	Original serial number	Chunk	Chinese translation	Corresponding rule	Standard score
196	117474	E117474 = sales confirmation	C117474 = 销售确认书	E117474 = C117474	100
197	118138	E118138 = opened in your favor	C118138 = 开立以你方为受益人	E118138 = C118138	100
198	120629	E120629 = ready for shipment	C120629 = 准备装船	E120629 = C120629	100
199	120779	E120779 = irrevocable letter of credit	C120779 = 不可撤销信用证	E120779 = C120779	100
200	121457	E121457 = prompt attention	C121457 = 及时关注	E121457 = C121457	100
201	121561	E121561 = sign and return one copy for our file	C121561 = 签署后退还一份以便存档	E121561 = C121561	100
202	122024	E122024 = have not yet received	C122024 = 尚未收到	E122024 = C122024	100
203	122926	E122926 = in reply to your letter	C122926 = 兹复你方来信	E122926 = C122926	100
204	123306	E123306 = do your utmost to	C123306 = 尽最大努力	E123306 = C123306	100
205	123314	E123314 = under the captioned contract	C123314 = 标题合同之下	E123314 = C123314	100
206	123681	E123681 = full set of shipping documents	C123681 = 全套装运单据	E123681 = C123681	100
207	124398	E124398 = additional saving on insurance	C124398 = 节省额外的保险	E124398 = C124398	100
208	124415	E124415 = carried in one container	C124415 = 装在同一集装箱	E124415 = C124415	100
209	124873	E124873 = shipping space has been fully booked up	C124873 = 舱位已经全部订满	E124873 = C124873	100
210	125311	E125311 = can be opened at both ends	C125311 = 两端均可打开	E125311 = C125311	100

(continued)

Table 4.50 (continued)

No.	Original serial number	Chunk	Chinese translation	Corresponding rule	Standard score
211	125354	E125354 = partial shipment	C125354 = 分批装运	E125354 = C125354	100
212	126122	E126122 = can be loaded and locked	C126122 = 既可装货又可封锁	E126122 = C126122	100
213	126626	E126626 = valid until	C126626 = 有效期至	E126626 = C126626	100
214	127043	E127043 = on a cash basis	C127043 = 现金方式	E127043 = C127043	100
215	128580	E128580 = brisk demand	C128580a = 旺盛的需求	① E128580 ≈ C128580a	80
			C128580b = 需求旺盛	② E128580 ≈ C128580b	20
216	128645	E128645 = very brisk demands	C128645 = 非常旺盛的需求	E128645 = C128645	100
217	130634	E130634 = name and address	C130634 = 名字和地址	E130634 = C130634	100
218	130655	E130655 = good reputation	C130655 = 良好声誉	E130655 = C130655	100
219	131380	E131380 = large quantities	C131380 = 大量	E131380 = C131380	100
220	132113	E132113 = supply from stock	C132113 = 提供现货	E132113 = C132113	100
221	132235	E132235 = settle their account directly	C132235 = 直接付款	E132235 = C132235	100
222	132443	E132443 = a full range of samples	C132443 = 一整套样品	E132443 = C132443	100
223	135671	E135671 = want to know	C135671a = 想了解	① E135671 ≈ C135671a	80
			C135671b = 想知道	② E135671 ≈ C135671b	20
224	135741	E135741 = reply at your earliest convenience	C135741 = 方便时尽早回复	E135741 = C135741	100
225	137956	E137956 = against all risks	C137956 = 投保一切险	E137956 = C137956	100
226	138991	E138991 = rate of premium	C138991 = 保险费率	E138991 = C138991	100

(continued)

Table 4.50 (continued)

No.	Original serial number	Chunk	Chinese translation	Corresponding rule	Standard score
227	139130	E139130 = under the policy	C139130 = 根据这一规定	E139130 = C139130	100
228	139132	E139132 = am writing to ask	C139132 = 致信询问	E139132 = C139132	100
229	140133	E140133 = thank you for your letter	C140133a = 多谢您……的来信	① E140133 ≈ C140133a	70
			C140133b = 谢谢您……的来信	② E140133 ≈ C140133b	16
			C140133c = 多谢您的来信	③ E140133 ≈ C140133c	9
			C140133d = 感谢您的来信	④ E140133 ≈ C140133d	5
230	140569	E140569 = above address	C140569 = 上述地址	E140569 = C140569	100
231	142813	E142813 = get in touch	C142813 = 取得联系	E142813 = C142813	100
232	144216	E144216 = upon receipt of	C144216 = 一旦收到	E144216 = C144216	100
233	144223	E144223 = most favorable price	C144223 = 最优惠价格	E144223 = C144223	100
234	144230	E144230 = within two months	C144230 = 两个月之内	E144230 = C144230	100
235	144234	E144234 = counter offer	C144234 = 还盘	E144234 = C144234	100
236	144249	E144249 = growing demand	C144249 = 不断增长的需求	E144249 = C144249	100
237	144309	E144309 = shipment to be made	C144309 = 装运	E144309 = C144309	100
238	146079	E146079 = find both quality and prices satisfactory	C146079a = 对产品质量和价格都非常满意	① E146079 ≈ C146079a	67
			C146079b = 对于品质和价格均感满意	② E146079 ≈ C146079b	33

(continued)

Table 4.50 (continued)

No.	Original serial number	Chunk	Chinese translation	Corresponding rule	Standard score
239	146700	E146700 = by the end of this month	C146700 = 本月底	E146700 = C146700	100
240	149386	E149386 = make this request	C149386a = 提出这个要求	① E149386 ≈ C149386a	80
			C149386b = 提出此要求	② E149386 ≈ C149386b	20
241	149882	E149882 = cancel part of the order	C149882 = 取消部分订单	E149882 = C149882	100
242	151624	E151624 = on the other hand	C151624 = 另一方面	E151624 = C151624	100
243	151675	E151675 = at the end of each month	C151675 = 每月月底	E151675 = C151675	100
244	152019	E152019 = formal agreement	C152019a = 正式合约	① E152019 ≈ C152019a	83
			C152019b = 正式协议	② E152019 ≈ C152019b	17
245	152929	E152929 = quite satisfactory	C152929 = 相当满意	E152929 = C152929	100

Table 4.51 Proportions of the three types of correspondence

Type	Quantity	Ratio/%
Complete correspondence	227	92.65
Incomplete correspondence	17	6.94
Zero correspondence	1	0.41
Sum	245	100

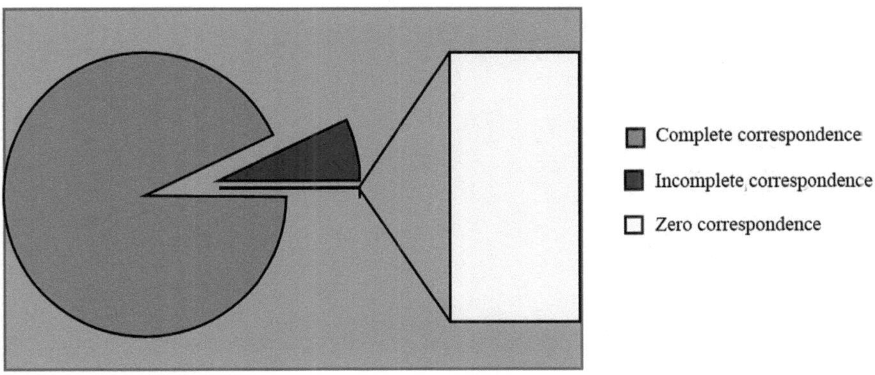

Fig. 4.2 Pie chart of the proportion of the three types of correspondence

complete correspondence, conducive to the MT of English-Chinese business letters, further improving the accuracy of translations. Chapter Five is a study on the construction mode of the MT-oriented corresponding chunk bank in English-Chinese business correspondences.

References

Lefevere, A. (1992). *Translation, rewriting, and the manipulation of literary fame*. Routledge.

Lu, J., & Wei, N. (2012). Study on the formation of equivalence patterns in English-Chinese translation based on extended sense unit model. *Foreign Language Teaching and Research, 3*, 424–436.

Teubert, W. (2002). The role of parallel corpora in translation and multilingual lexicography. In B. Altenberg & S. Granger (Eds.), *Lexis in contrast—Corpus-based approaches* (pp. 189–214). John Benjamins Publishing Company.

Chapter 5
Construction Mode and Application of a Chunk Bank

5.1 Introduction

In this chapter, we conduct a study on the construction mode of the MT-oriented corresponding chunk bank in English-Chinese business correspondences, which can effectively carry out the construction of chunk banks in various fields. At the same time, this chapter also looks into the application prospect of chunk banks in MT.

5.2 Construction Mode of a Chunk Bank

The construction mode of the chunk bank is based on the MT-oriented study of corresponding lexical chunks in business correspondences from English to Chinese, providing a pattern for the construction of a large-scale corpus-based MT-oriented corresponding chunk bank in English-Chinese business correspondences. It can also be applied to texts in other fields, such as contract texts, tourism texts, law texts, etc. Not a regulation, the mode is a process of building a chunk bank through various modules and methods. Its programming and modularization aim to effectively build chunk banks in various fields, so as to finally form a large-scale general chunk bank that encompasses all fields and serves English-Chinese machine translation systems. In this sense, the significance of the construction mode of chunk banks for MT is self-evident.

A. Three levels

In this chapter, the construction mode of a chunk bank contains three level, including the basic resources level, the man–machine interactive extraction level, and the corresponding rules level, as shown in Fig. 5.1.

a. The basic resources level

F. Hu, *An MT-Oriented Study of Corresponding Lexical Chunks in Business Correspondences from English to Chinese*,
https://doi.org/10.1007/978-981-99-4977-9_5

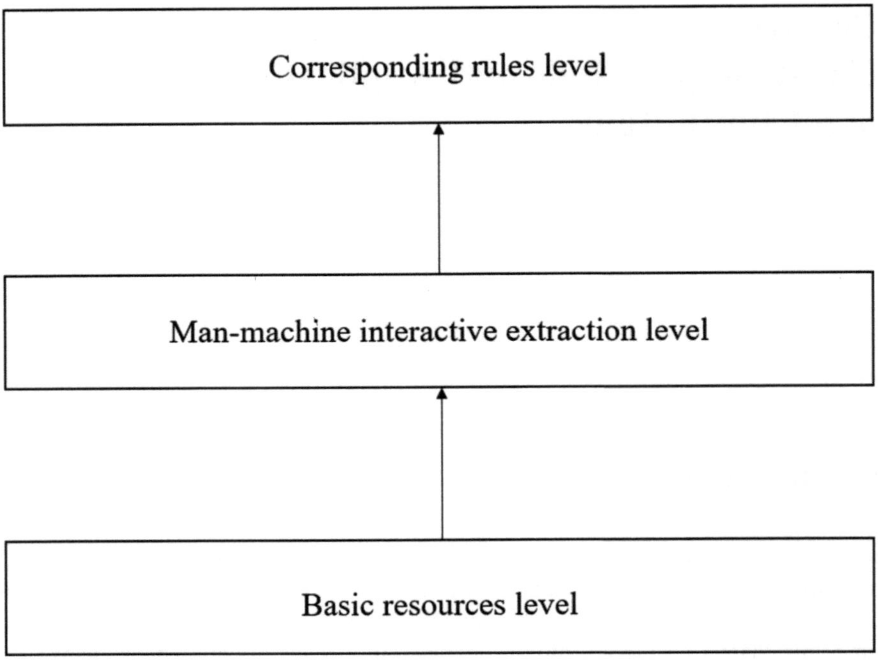

Fig. 5.1 Three levels of the construction mode of chunk banks

The basic resources level mainly refers to the English-Chinese business correspondences parallel corpus, which is the basis of the construction mode of the MT-oriented corresponding chunk bank in English-Chinese business correspondences. When building the corpus, we should pay attention to three principles: ① The selected corpus should be of high translation quality, and the business correspondences published by regular publishers are priorities, instead of online informal materials, for the accuracy of online linguistic data is not enough and its translation quality varies. Therefore, published textbooks and works are undoubtedly reliable sources of bilingual corpus. ② The classification of the corpus should be clear, and the corpus should be collected representatively and extensively as much as possible. ③ Rely on existing software to achieve automatic alignment at the level of discourse and sentence, and then perform manual proofreading.

b. The man–machine interactive extraction level

This level is mainly concerned with the human–computer interactive extraction of the corresponding chunks in business English correspondences. The format of the discourse-aligned letters needs to be converted to accommodate to the corpus phrase extraction system. The sentence-aligned letters and the corresponding Chinese versions are then imported into Microsoft Word and Excel respectively, so that the corresponding chunks as well as its translations in the parallel corpus can be retrieved. Candidate chunks are automatically extracted using the corpus phrase extraction system, and those that do not meet the criteria for the definition of the MT-oriented chunks in business English correspondences are then manually removed to obtain the final chunks.

c. The corresponding rules level

At this level, the retrieval function in ParaConc is mainly used to retrieve the MT-oriented chunks in business English letters. The MT-oriented business English letter chunks and corresponding example sentences are searched and further analyzed in order to summarize their corresponding relationship and rules, set down corresponding rules and standard scores, and develop the MT-oriented corresponding chunk bank in English-Chinese business letters. The above three levels constitute the macro-operation process and the following describes the six modules at the three levels, which belong to the micro-operation process.

B. Six modules

In the three levels of the construction mode of chunk banks, six modules are designed, which are the text preprocessing module, the automatic extraction module, the manual processing module, the corresponding relations module, the corresponding rules formulation module, and the standard score evaluation module. Among them, the man–machine interactive extraction level includes the text preprocessing module, the automatic extraction module, the manual processing module; the corresponding rules level includes the corresponding relations module, the corresponding rules formulation module, and the standard score evaluation module. In this way, the flow chart of the construction mode of the MT-oriented corresponding chunk bank in English-Chinese business correspondences is finally built, as shown in Fig. 5.2.

a. The text preprocessing module

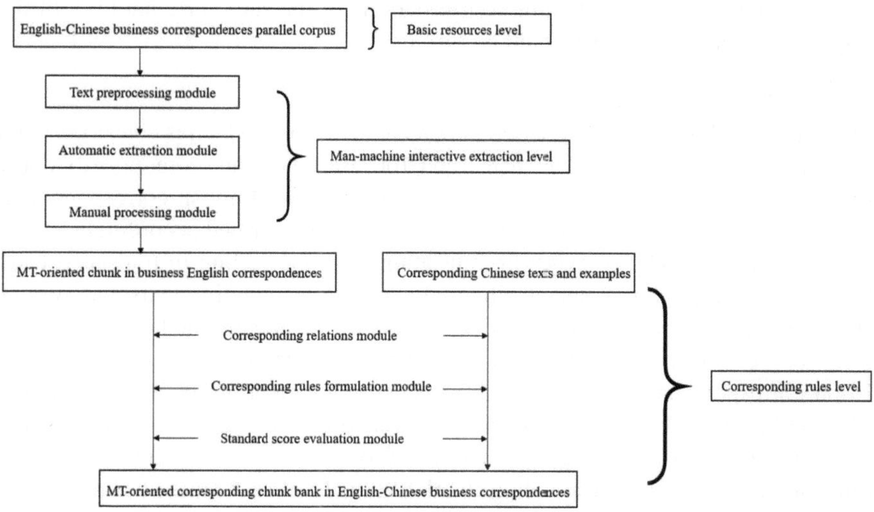

Fig. 5.2 Flowchart of construction mode of chunk banks

At this stage, we rename the file names of the discourse and sentence aligned business English letters and the corresponding Chinese letters, using 1_E, 2_E, 3_E, ..., N_E for English and 1_C, 2_C, 3_C, ..., N_C for Chinese. Then the format is converted from TXT to UTF-8, meeting the requirement of phrase extraction.

b. The automatic extraction module

With the help of the chunk extraction system, the *N*-grams in business English letters are automatically extracted according to 2–9 g, and Grams with a frequency of more than 2 are kept after automatic de-emphasis processing. Calculated by the MI method, and candidate chunks are finally obtained.

c. The manual processing module

Candidate chunks that do not meet the definition of an MT-oriented chunk in business English correspondences are manually removed.

d. The corresponding relations module

By observing the MT-oriented corresponding chunks in English-Chinese business letters and the example sentences in the parallel corpus, it is found that the correspondence could be divided into three types: complete correspondence, incomplete correspondence and zero correspondence. The symbols of the three correspondences are "=" for complete correspondence, "≈" for incomplete correspondence, and "*" for zero correspondence.

e. The corresponding rules formulation module

In this study, "E" stands for the MT-oriented chunks in business English correspondences while "C" for the corresponding Chinese translations. The original serial number is a unique code automatically assigned by the chunk extraction system in order to find the original sentence in the text. In the incomplete correspondence, "a, b, c, ..." indicates different Chinese translations of the same original text. In this way, the corresponding rules could be formulated.

f. The standard score evaluation module

The corresponding ratio is expressed in percent (1–100%), which is converted to the standard score with a range between 1 and 100. Based on the score, priority correspondence matching of MT-oriented chunks in business English correspondences and their corresponding Chinese translations will be performed accordingly.

Translation knowledge exists in translation facts indwelling in translated texts. By collecting a large number of bilingual chunk corresponding texts and systematic descriptions of translation facts, the probabilistic statistic methods are used to discover recurring chunk translation corresponding units in order to establish translation correspondence (Li, 2010). MT-oriented corresponding chunks in English-Chinese business correspondences are researched to achieve the maximum correspondence to the original language in terms of form, semantics and function. Therefore, the MT-oriented corresponding chunk bank in English-Chinese business correspondences, composed of chunks in business English correspondences as well as its Chinese translations, provides a rich translation knowledge base for the computer.

Another point is direction of translation/ directionality. Lonsdale (2004/1988) gave a definition as "whether translators are working from a foreign language into their mother tongue or vice versa". The mode of the MT-oriented corresponding chunk bank in English-Chinese business correspondences designed in this book is from English to Chinese, and for the time being, it does not involve C-E direction. This research aims to provide theoretical support, technology and method for the MT-oriented corresponding chunk bank in English-Chinese business correspondences, thus improving the English-Chinese business correspondence MT system. If the Chinese-English business correspondence MT system is carried out in the future, the chunk bank in C-E direction will be further studied.

In summary, this book conducts a study on the construction mode of the MT-oriented corresponding chunk banks in English-Chinese business correspondences, which is divided into three levels: the basic resources level, the man–machine interactive extraction level, and the corresponding rules level. Specifically, they are composed of six modules, including the text preprocessing module, the automatic extraction module, the manual processing module, the corresponding relations module, the corresponding rules formulation module, and the standard score evaluation module. The application prospects of MT-oriented chunk banks for machine translation are presented in the next section.

5.3 Application Prospects

In the 1980s, some scholars proposed a MT approach based on corpus, which requires large-scale bilingual corpora that are mutually translated. It is divided into the example-based MT and the statistics-based MT, both of them is of great importance to the chunk correspondence, because the corpora that has undergone chunk correspondence is an extremely valuable source of translation knowledge.

The MT-oriented corresponding chunk bank in English-Chinese business correspondences stores a large number of corresponding chunks, which can be used in the English-Chinese business correspondences MT system to solve communication barriers and promote domestic and foreign trade and economic exchanges. MT is mainly applied in three areas: work for which rough translation is sufficient, post-editing or "human-aided MT", and translation in restricted sub-language fields that can produce high-quality translations (Feng, 2004). In recent years, the role of bilingual corresponding chunk banks in research and development of MT has been increasingly recognized. Researchers have proposed a variety of new approaches such as example-based methods, statistics-based methods, and storage-based methods, which not only improve the quality of automatic machine translations by directly using the corresponding bilingual chunk bank, but also enhance the human–computer interaction in machine-assisted translation.

Therefore, the MT-oriented corresponding chunk bank in English-Chinese business correspondences will certainly improve the accuracy of MT systems.

(1) The machine translation based on the MT-oriented corresponding chunk bank in English-Chinese business correspondences is precisely an attempt to overcome the shortcomings of traditional systems and improve the efficiency and accuracy of translation. Starting from lexical chunks instead of individual words, this attempt not only eliminates ambiguities, but also greatly improves the translation efficiency. Only by effectively incorporating language knowledge and translation knowledge, especially bilingual corresponding chunks, into MT, can the accuracy be improved to a higher level.
(2) The construction mode of the MT-oriented corresponding chunk bank in English-Chinese business correspondences is programmed and modularized through various modules and methods, aiming at effectively constructing bilingual corresponding chunk bank for each limited field, such as materials, electronics, mining, metallurgy, machinery, aviation, tourism, etc., so as to finally form a large-scale general chunk bank that encompasses all fields and serves English-Chinese machine translation systems. In addition, the mode designed in this study is dynamic, and with the continuous collection of the relevant corpus, it is believed that the chunk bank will be constantly expanded and updated. As the number of bilingual corresponding chunks stored increases, more and more problems in MT will be eventually solved.
(3) In the machine-assisted translation system, the use of the MT-oriented corresponding chunk bank in English-Chinese business correspondences can improve the consistency and standardization of translations, which can save time and promote the translation efficiency. After the bilingual corresponding chunk bank in various fields is finished, the fully automatic and high-quality MT system will greatly boost the translation accuracy and better serve translations.

The author has tested current mainstream translation tool softwares and found that the error of relatively high frequency is that the recognition of translation objects is based on words rather than chunks, leading to chunks being split into smaller language units, usually smaller phrases or words than chunks. Therefore, theoretically, an MT-oriented corresponding chunk bank in English-Chinese business correspondences will definitely boost the accuracy of MT.

To verify the effectiveness in practice, this chapter uses the WordFast Classic to conduct a translation comparison experiments on the basis of 200 business English letters randomly selected from the remaining 90% of the English-Chinese business correspondence parallel corpus and the corresponding 200 business Chinese letters as the experimental objects.

(1) Input 200 business English letters directly into WordFast Classic and translate them into Chinese.
(2) Under the mode proposed in this chapter, 200 E-C corresponding business letters are extracted and a table of corresponding chunks in E-C business correspondences was produced, which are then input into the translation memory database of WordFast Classic. Next, the above 200 business English letters are input into the software to be translated into Chinese.
(3) Compare the translation quality by analysis.

The results show that the translation quality of experiment (2) is significantly higher than that of experiment (1). Examples are given below. (The bolded part is the extracted corresponding chunk.)

原文: As you may not be aware of **the wide range of goods we deal in**, we are enclosing a copy of our catalogue and hope that our handing of your first order with us will lead to further business between us and mark the beginning of a happy working relationship.

译文: 您也许对我公司经营的货物范围不太了解, 现附上目录一份, 希望自此订单开始, 彼此建立更多的业务来往, 展开愉快的工作关系。

(WordFast Classic 对语块 "the wide range of goods we deal in" 的翻译为: 我们经营的范围广泛的产品。).

原文: We **find both quality and prices satisfactory** and are pleased to give you an order for the following items on the understanding that they will be supplied from current stock at the price names.

译文: 我公司对于品质和价格均感满意, 更乐意在指定价格及供应现货的条件下订购下列货物。

(WordFast Classic 对语块 "find both quality and prices satisfactory" 的翻译为: 找到满意的质量和价格。).

原文: **Please send us your proforma invoice in triplicate** and we shall be ready to place an order for 10,000 dozen slippers with you.

译文: 请寄给我们一式三份的形式发票, 我们将给您下一万打拖鞋的订单。

(WordFast Classic 对语块 "please send us your proforma invoice in triplicate" 的翻译为: 请寄给我们形式发票你的一式三份。).

It proves that the MT-oriented corresponding chunk bank in E-C business correspondences plays an important role and can effectively improve the quality of MT.

5.4 Summary

The construction mode of the MT-oriented corresponding chunk bank in E-C business correspondences includes three levels: the basic resources level, the man–machine interactive extraction level, and the corresponding rules level. The basic resources level is mainly the E-C business correspondence parallel corpus, which is the basis of the construction mode. The man–machine interactive extraction level includes the text preprocessing module, the automatic extraction module, the manual processing module, which is monolingual (referring to English in this chapter). The corresponding rules level includes the corresponding relations module, the corresponding rules formulation module, and the standard score evaluation module, which is bilingual (referring to E-C in this chapter). As for the application prospects, it is expected to effectively build chunk banks in various fields, so as to finally form a large-scale general chunk bank that encompasses all fields and serves E-C machine translation systems, which would play a crucial role in improving the translation accuracy of E-C business correspondence machine translation system.

References

Feng, Z. (2004). *Machine translation.* China Translation & Publishing Corporation.

Li, W. (2010). Design of parallel corpus and identification of corresponding units. *Contemporary Foreign Languages Studies, 9*, 22–27.

Lonsdale, A. B. (2004/1988). Direction of translation (Directionality). In B. Mona (Ed.), *Routledge encyclopedia of translation studies* (pp. 63–75). Routledge.

Conclusion

Liu (1997: 81–82), an expert in machine translation at the Institute of Linguistics, Chinese Academy of Social Sciences, points out that even the software and hardware technology of computers is good, the level of machine translation will not be advanced if the quality of machine dictionaries based on low quality linguistic knowledge in his article *Machine translation is ultimately a linguistic problem* published in *Applied Linguistics*. He emphasizes that we should conduct more comparative linguistic research and summarizing the experience of human translation is the most urgent task, and suggests using the fixed structure in language[1] to exclude multiple meanings as well as to improve the quality and speed of translation. Liu (2009: 157), an expert in statistical machine translation at the Institute of Computing Technology, Chinese Academy of Sciences, points out that some machine translation problems cannot really be solved without introducing more complex linguistic knowledge in his article *New Progress in Machine Translation Research* in *Current Linguistics*. Both articles point out the importance of linguistic knowledge and translation knowledge for machine translation.

The main obstacles that affect the quality of machine translation systems are the processing of ambiguity and the use of common-sense knowledge (Li, 2013: 381). Traditional machine translation does not give sufficient consideration to context. As we all know, words are often polysemous. So far, there is no reliable method to remove lexical ambiguity yet, especially for two unrelated languages like English and Chinese, which is not easy to be removed lexical ambiguity in translation. In addition, translation practice proves that people do not translate word by word without context, but consider words as meaning units that are large enough to be unambiguous, that is, the combination of several words[2] as a translation unit (Teubert & Čermakova, 2004/145).

[1] A chunk is a kind of fixed structure, and from the perspective of machine translation, a chunk is a granular unit suitable for translation matching.

[2] The author thinks it refers to the language block.

F. Hu, *An MT-Oriented Study of Corresponding Lexical Chunks in Business Correspondences from English to Chinese*,
https://doi.org/10.1007/978-981-99-4977-9

Li (2010: 22) proposes the concept of corresponding units, which corresponds to any identifiable text block or fragment in the source text and the destination text. The corresponding units have integrity and identity in meaning, and have their own syntactic structural features. However, Li and Zhao (2013: 37) believe that any identifiable text block or fragment does not strictly restrict the language class of the corresponding unit. Theoretically speaking, text translation at word level, phrase level, sentence level and even larger level can be regarded as the corresponding unit, which not only blurs the characteristics of the corresponding unit, but also increases the difficulty of recognition and extraction.

Pu (2014: 53–61) makes a comparative analysis of translation units, meaning units and corresponding units from the perspective of corpus-driven translation studies. The unit of meaning breaks the previous concept of single word as the core and basic unit of meaning, and establishes a new language unit that is oriented by meaning function, determined by use (i.e. constructed by discourse community), dominated by multi-word combination, and has certain variability in form.[3] Translation unit is the smallest and single meaning in the source language, and there can only be synonymous translation equivalent language units in the target language. The corresponding units mainly consider the units below the sentence, and refer to the reasonable factors in the definition of translation units, and reposition in the framework of meaning units. The unit of meaning is an extended unit, which contains not only the topic, but also the corresponding attitude meaning. The combination of these forms a stable and complete combination of formal structure and meaning function.[4] If we can grasp the meaning of the unit in translation, then to achieve faithfulness and expressiveness is not so far away.

Li and Zhao (2013: 36–40) study the recognition and application of corresponding word sequences in the newly built parallel corpus of Shanghai Jiao Tong University. They find that there is a large amount of word sequence translation equivalence in parallel texts, covering collocations, compound words, idioms, fixed and semi-fixed phrases, as well as a large number of incomplete word fragments and other complex language forms. Therefore, they put forward the concept of corresponding word sequence for academic English texts, focusing on the translation equivalence of word sequence, and the corpus is an annotated parallel corpus of Shanghai Jiao Tong University. At the end of the paper, they point out that corresponding word sequence is still an operational concept, and some identification criteria need to be more strictly defined. During the process of the construction of corpus, they find that both theory of monolingual and bilingual research, meaning to realize the main carrier is the expression of words sequence type. These language units and their translation counterparts appear frequently, and some even become fixed translations. It embodies the cross-language text constitute characteristics of communication, and

[3] The author thinks that it is equivalent to language block.

[4] According to the understanding of construction grammar, construction refers to the combination of form and meaning/function. The author holds that constructions consist of words and blocks respectively, and blocks consist of words collocation and combination, and blocks are a special kind of constructions. Thus, blocks are also a combination of form and meaning/function.

this will become a new hotspot in the research of the future comparative language. Therefore, machine translation based on bilingual corresponding blocks is an attempt to overcome the shortcomings of traditional machine translation systems and further improve the accuracy of machine translation systems.

Blocks are the most preferred units for machine translation and language teaching because they are easy to extract and enable the speaker to pay attention to the language structure of larger units. McAlpine and Myles (2003: 71–84) proposes: First, compile a dictionary. The entry takes node words as the core, and lists related blocks and common collocation patterns around node words with example sentences, so that learners can learn the general background and collocation knowledge about the word, but this idea has not been realized so far. Second, the machine aided translation software is developed by using language blocks, and the computer realizes bilingual conversion by processing language blocks. Therefore, in addition to machine translation, the research of bilingual corresponding chunk bank can also compile a human–machine universal bilingual block dictionary. The entries are arranged in the order of the original sequence number of the block, and the corresponding sentences of the block and their corresponding rules and standard scores of the Chinese translation. This kind of dictionary is not only beneficial to English teaching, but also can serve the computer for machine translation, information retrieval and so on.

This book first proposes the construction, language block (word), a theoretical model of block formation analysis, by the theory of construction grammar. The definition and definition standard of business English chunk bank for machine translation are analyzed. Secondly, it extracts the chunks of business English letters based on the human–computer interaction of parallel corpora, and develops the corresponding chunks table of English and Chinese business letters. Thirdly, the correspondence relations and corresponding rules of English and Chinese business letter blocks for machine translation are analyzed. Finally, the paper discusses the construction model and application prospect of the corresponding language block library of English-Chinese business letters for machine translation.

To be specific, this book gives full play to the interdisciplinary advantages, pays attention to the practical principle, and uses the method of combining qualitative analysis and quantitative analysis to conduct in-depth research from four aspects.

First, from the perspective of construction grammar theory, based on the thinking of construction grammar theory and the study of blocks, the theoretical model of block composition analysis is put forward to define blocks, which provides theoretical support for the study of this book.

Second, through the three levels of text preprocessing, automatic extraction, and manual processing, we realize human–computer interaction based on parallel corpora business English letter language block extraction. The extraction of business English chunk banks based on parallel corpora and human–computer interaction is the key technology to develop the corresponding block library of English-Chinese business letters for machine translation.

Third, this book analyzes the correspondence between the chunks of business English letters for machine translation and their corresponding Chinese translations, and formulates their corresponding rules and standard scores. At the same time, it makes a table of the chunks of English-Chinese business letters for machine translation, which provides some basic resources for the construction of the MT-oriented study of corresponding lexical chunks in business correspondences from English to Chinese, which can serve the English-Chinese business letter machine translation system, so as to further improve the translation accuracy of English-Chinese business letter machine translation system.

Fourthly, this book studies the construction model of bilingual corresponding language block bank. The process construction of this model can form a large-scale lingua franca block bank, which will play a certain role in improving the accuracy of machine translation system.

The innovations of this book is as follows: ① The theoretical model of block construction analysis is proposed by the theory of construction grammar, and the chunks of business English letters for machine translation are defined, which provides theoretical support for the development of MT-oriented corresponding chunk bank in English-Chinese business correspondences. ② We realize the extraction of business English letter chunks based on human–computer interaction based on parallel corpora, and provide technical support for the development of MT-oriented corresponding chunk bank in English-Chinese business correspondences. ③ Analysis for machine translation of English business letter forms corresponding relation and corresponding rules, and develop corresponding forms piece of table and construction mode for MT-oriented corresponding chunk bank in English-Chinese business correspondences, in order to provide methods of large-scale development for MT-oriented corresponding chunk bank in English-Chinese business correspondences.

References

Li, W. (2010). Design of parallel corpus and identification of corresponding units. *Contemporary Foreign Languages Studies, 9*, 22–27.

Li, S. (2013). Research and development in natural language processing. *Journal of Yanshan University (Philosophy and Social Science Edition), 5*, 376–384.

Li, J., & Zhao, X. (2013). Research on recognition and application of corresponding word sequences in parallel texts. *Technology Enhanced Foreign Languages, 5*, 36–40.

Liu, Y. (1997). Machine translation is essentially a linguistic problem. *Applied Linguistics, 3*, 81–82.

Liu, Q. (2009). Recent advances in machine translation research. *Contemporary Linguistics, 2*, 147–158.

McAlpine, J., & Myles, J. (2003). Capturing phraseology in an online dictionary for advanced users of English as a second language: A response to user needs. *System, 31*, 71–84.

Pu, J. (2003). Collocation, connection, and lexical chunks in English vocabulary teaching. *Foreign Language Teaching and Research, 6*, 438–445.

Teubert, W., & Čermáková, A. (2004). Directions in corpus linguistics. In M. A. K. Halliday et al. (Eds.), *Lexicology and corpus linguistics*. Continuum.

Appendix
Candidate Language Chunks Automatically Extracted by Computer

There are 290 candidate blocks automatically extracted by the computer in this book. After the software extracts the words, they are all lowercase and sorted by the original sequence number from the smallest to the largest, so as to view the relevant original example sentences in the text.

Sequence number	Original sequence number	Candidate blocks	Number of N	Frequency
1	2529	lead to further business between us	6	3
2	2582	certainly do our best to make it so	8	3
3	3827	dear sir or madam	4	6
4	4301	allow you a discount	4	3
5	4798	working relationship	2	3
6	5123	contract to be drawn up	5	3
7	6003	pleased to enclose our order no.	6	3
8	8287	quite willing to undertake the training	6	3
9	9986	present salary	2	3
10	10007	only reason	2	3
11	10893	a sole agency for marketing	5	3
12	13310	serve you well	3	3
13	14440	past four years	3	4
14	16721	representative selection	2	4
15	17093	at an early date	4	9
16	17510	a wide range of	4	5

(continued)

F. Hu, *An MT-Oriented Study of Corresponding Lexical Chunks in Business Correspondences from English to Chinese*,
https://doi.org/10.1007/978-981-99-4977-9

(continued)

Sequence number	Original sequence number	Candidate blocks	Number of N	Frequency
17	17522	many thanks for your quotation	5	3
18	17529	be glad to learn	4	5
19	17652	poor condition	2	4
20	20079	office manager	2	3
21	20567	make clear beforehand	3	3
22	20775	packed in international standard	4	3
23	21108	which the port of destination and our order number	9	3
24	21662	reach you in good time	5	4
25	22537	early decision	2	3
26	22689	local conditions	2	3
27	23485	regret to tell you	4	3
28	23504	goods are shipped	3	4
29	23687	no available space	3	4
30	24065	an early reply will be obliged	6	3
31	24782	prompt reply will be greatly appreciated	6	3
32	25398	be willing to establish business relations with us	8	3
33	27018	defer payment for a further three weeks	7	3
34	27160	defer payment	2	3
35	28885	cash discount	2	4
36	28936	in full settlement	3	5
37	29315	pleased to inform	3	14
38	29853	sole agents	2	3
39	30780	payment of the balance	4	3
40	32046	commercial bank of hong kong	5	3
41	32170	good enough	2	6
42	32359	commercial bank of shanghai	4	3
43	33751	until the end of this year	6	3

(continued)

(continued)

Sequence number	Original sequence number	Candidate blocks	Number of N	Frequency
44	35160	apply for an overdraft	4	3
45	36586	both surprised and disappointed	4	3
46	37516	a trial period of twelve months	6	3
47	38557	entirely satisfactory	2	4
48	40791	date of invoice	3	3
49	40917	these prices include packing and delivery	6	3
50	41881	small profit	2	3
51	42198	welcome the opportunity to do business with you	8	3
52	42463	special discount	2	4
53	42553	prices we quoted	3	5
54	42649	sorry to learn from your letter	6	3
55	43711	forced to cut our prices to the minimum	8	3
56	43795	having carefully considered	3	3
57	44317	feel confident	2	3
58	44950	find a ready sale	4	3
59	45163	a ready sale for our products in your market	9	3
60	45260	an exceptional case	3	3
61	45418	convince you of the reasonableness of our quotation	8	3
62	45512	a fair comparison of quality	6	3
63	46104	interested in our proposal	4	3
64	46811	provide a guarantor	3	3
65	47560	on going into the matter	5	7
66	47600	right goods to be dispatched	5	3
67	47611	dispatched to you at once	5	3

(continued)

(continued)

Sequence number	Original sequence number	Candidate blocks	Number of N	Frequency
68	47614	relative documents will be mailed	5	3
69	48722	look forward to receiving your further orders	7	3
70	50911	sole agency	2	10
71	53728	due to arrive	3	4
72	54550	sales promotion	2	3
73	55092	saving in freight charges	4	3
74	55248	the shipping containers we provide	5	3
75	55417	load and unload at the same time	7	3
76	56358	a thousand tons	3	3
77	57451	sent herewith	2	4
78	57490	damaged during transit	3	4
79	57584	regret to note that	4	3
80	57601	clean bill of lading	4	4
81	57604	your claim on order	4	3
82	57658	claim to be lodged	4	4
83	57716	suggest you set out a claim immediately	7	4
84	57722	hope our explanation will be satisfactory	6	4
85	57732	a claim immediately against the shipping company	7	4
86	57754	have received your letter of april	6	4
87	57781	good condition when they left here	6	4
88	57893	goods in question were carefully packed by experienced workmen	9	4
89	58084	unpacking the cases	3	4
90	58094	requirements of this market	4	4
91	58194	must return the goods to you	6	4

(continued)

(continued)

Sequence number	Original sequence number	Candidate blocks	Number of N	Frequency
92	58199	look forward to your early settlement	6	4
93	58232	found that the quality was not satisfactory	7	4
94	58246	for the invoice value and inspection charges involved	8	4
95	58254	regret to inform you	4	4
96	58258	the survey report issued by beijing commodity inspection bureau	9	3
97	58296	not up to the standard of samples	7	4
98	58298	the goods delivered is not up to the standard	9	4
99	58328	too inferior to be suitable for the requirements	8	4
100	58427	prepared to consider	3	3
101	58930	shipping documents	2	10
102	58999	completely different articles	3	3
103	59930	regular customers	2	5
104	60086	comply with your request	4	5
105	60262	have no choice but to do so	7	3
106	61052	through a confusion of number	5	3
107	61193	did not contain the goods you ordered	7	3
108	61227	a mistake is indeed made in the packing	8	3
109	61364	dress materials supplied	3	4
110	61400	after careful examination	3	3
111	61511	duly received the documents	4	4
112	62195	sincere apologies	2	3
113	63651	kindly requested	2	3

(continued)

(continued)

Sequence number	Original sequence number	Candidate blocks	Number of N	Frequency
114	64061	settle the problem	3	3
115	65279	many thanks for your letter	5	3
116	66000	please let me know	4	4
117	67951	reduction in your price	4	3
118	68030	enclosed herewith	2	3
119	68443	draw your attention	3	3
120	68762	price lists	2	3
121	68799	various types	2	3
122	68807	iron nails	2	3
123	68930	above will be acceptable to you	6	3
124	69685	last year	2	3
125	71210	last week	2	3
126	71950	transaction prove to be successful	5	3
127	72467	in urgent need of these goods	6	3
128	72496	make delivery at an early date	6	3
129	73625	please send us your proforma invoice in triplicate	8	3
130	73731	within the contracted time	4	3
131	74102	the delivery date is approaching	5	3
132	74449	above mentioned	2	5
133	77261	two years ago	3	4
134	77426	the said license is approved	5	3
135	78045	in this particular line of business	6	3
136	79410	san francisco	2	4
137	80714	enter into business	3	3
138	80835	one of the leading importers	5	3
139	81040	mutually beneficial	2	3
140	81560	bank of china	3	4

(continued)

(continued)

Sequence number	Original sequence number	Candidate blocks	Number of N	Frequency
141	81998	many years experience in this particular line of business	9	3
142	82341	the people's insurance company of china	6	4
143	83754	shipping advice	2	8
144	83798	due to sail	3	3
145	83853	end of this month	4	11
146	84635	meet with your approval	4	3
147	85611	debit note	2	4
148	88255	look forward to your early reply	6	13
149	88425	cotton sweaters	2	4
150	88805	our offer remains valid for one month	7	3
151	88878	under separate cover	3	4
152	88933	with keen interest	3	4
153	89250	per hundred	2	4
154	89293	from date of invoice	4	3
155	90087	indeed sorry that you found our price too high	9	3
156	90147	place regular and substantial orders	5	3
157	90177	have quoted such low prices	5	3
158	90610	to place a trial order	5	3
159	90653	hope you will reconsider	4	3
160	90682	such being the case	4	3
161	90695	accept your quotation would mean little profit	7	3
162	90756	all the terms contained in the offer are acceptable	9	3
163	90769	contained in the offer are acceptable except the price	9	3
164	90771	hope you will reconsider this matter	6	3

(continued)

(continued)

Sequence number	Original sequence number	Candidate blocks	Number of N	Frequency
165	90835	place more substantial orders on a regular basis	8	3
166	91051	must stress	2	4
167	91298	push the sales of	4	3
168	91311	quantity discount	2	3
169	91356	thank you for your inquiry	5	4
170	92845	claim form	2	3
171	93385	lower than	2	4
172	95401	in wooden cases	3	3
173	95582	packed in cartons	3	4
174	96055	do not hesitate to let us know	7	3
175	96467	mutual benefit	2	3
176	97377	keep dry	2	4
177	97450	order number should be stenciled	5	3
178	97635	paper bags	2	3
179	98959	warning marks	2	3
180	99006	in an fcl container	4	3
181	99196	be packed in international standard tea	6	3
182	99455	on the outer packing please mark our initials	8	3
183	99610	ocean transportation	2	3
184	100362	thank you in advance for your cooperation	7	4
185	101838	please see to it that	5	5
186	101893	avoid subsequent amendments	3	3
187	102340	hope to hear favorably from you	6	3
188	102522	time of shipment	3	5
189	102608	usual terms of payment	4	3
190	102695	by draft at sight	4	5
191	102894	look forward to the pleasure of your order	8	3

(continued)

(continued)

Sequence number	Original sequence number	Candidate blocks	Number of N	Frequency
192	103042	laser printer	2	6
193	103797	date and place of expiry	5	3
194	104190	so that we can	4	6
195	104294	national city bank of new york	6	3
196	104709	early reply will be highly appreciated	6	3
197	105009	favorable reply	2	6
198	106632	date of delivery	3	3
199	107015	payment by confirmed and irrevocable letter of credit	8	3
200	108544	less than	2	3
201	108547	usual practice	2	5
202	108879	good prospects	2	5
203	111579	well aware	2	3
204	113157	other suppliers	2	5
205	113189	quotation sheet	2	3
206	113720	illustrated catalogues	2	3
207	114413	may rest assured	3	4
208	114560	cfr basis	2	4
209	114797	early as possible by direct steamer to hong kong	9	3
210	114880	in due course	3	3
211	115058	not later than	3	5
212	115204	special care	2	3
213	115450	terms of payment	3	16
214	115471	latest catalogue	2	4
215	115480	satisfied with the quality	4	3
216	115505	in the near future	4	7
217	115506	within the next month	4	4
218	116751	per dozen	2	11
219	116774	maintain friendly relations	3	3
220	117192	drawn up	2	4

(continued)

(continued)

Sequence number	Original sequence number	Candidate blocks	Number of N	Frequency
221	117310	the wide range of goods we deal in	8	3
222	117328	enclosing a copy of our catalogue	6	3
223	117358	be aware of the wide range of goods	8	3
224	117474	sales confirmation	2	16
225	118138	opened in your favor	4	3
226	120629	ready for shipment	3	4
227	120779	irrevocable letter of credit	4	13
228	121457	prompt attention	2	5
229	121561	sign and return one copy for our file	8	3
230	122024	have not yet received	4	3
231	122272	selling season	2	4
232	122926	in reply to your letter	5	3
233	123306	do your utmost to	4	4
234	123314	under the captioned contract	4	4
235	123681	full set of shipping documents	5	3
236	124398	additional saving on insurance	4	3
237	124415	carried in one container	4	3
238	124873	shipping space has been fully booked up	7	3
239	124932	hong kong	2	18
240	125311	can be opened at both ends	6	3
241	125354	partial shipment	2	5
242	126122	can be loaded and locked	5	3
243	126626	valid until	2	6
244	127043	on a cash basis	4	4
245	128546	silk blouses	2	6
246	128580	brisk demand	2	5
247	128645	very brisk demands	3	3

(continued)

(continued)

Sequence number	Original sequence number	Candidate blocks	Number of N	Frequency
248	129266	light industrial products	3	3
249	130634	name and address	3	5
250	130655	good reputation	2	3
251	131380	large quantities	2	6
252	131387	electronic products	2	4
253	132113	supply from stock	3	3
254	132235	settle their account directly	4	3
255	132443	a full range of samples	5	3
256	134170	plastic furniture	2	4
257	135671	want to know	3	5
258	135741	reply at your earliest convenience	5	3
259	137039	window frames	2	4
260	137956	against all risks	3	5
261	138991	rate of premium	3	3
262	139130	under the policy	3	3
263	139132	am writing to ask	4	3
264	139885	more than	2	7
265	140048	at the same time	4	8
266	140133	thank you for your letter	5	43
267	140569	above address	2	7
268	140614	terms and conditions	3	12
269	142813	get in touch	3	3
270	143115	frying pan	2	4
271	144216	upon receipt of	3	13
272	144223	most favorable price	3	3
273	144230	within two months	3	3
274	144232	new york	2	16
275	144234	counter offer	2	7
276	144249	growing demand	2	3
277	144264	cif new york	3	4
278	144309	shipment to be made	4	4
279	146079	find both quality and prices satisfactory	6	3
280	146495	bill of exchange	3	3

(continued)

(continued)

Sequence number	Original sequence number	Candidate blocks	Number of N	Frequency
281	146700	by the end of this month	6	3
282	149386	make this request	3	5
283	149815	swimming trousers	2	4
284	149882	cancel part of the order	5	3
285	151624	on the other hand	4	3
286	151675	at the end of each month	6	3
287	152019	formal agreement	2	6
288	152860	bill of lading	3	12
289	152929	quite satisfactory	2	4
290	154276	as soon as possible	4	26

Bibliography

Cowan, N. (2000). The magical number 4 in short-term memory: A reconsideration of mental storage capacity. *Behavioral and Brain Sciences, 24*(1), 87–185.

Li, W. (2010). Design of parallel corpus and identification of corresponding units. *Contemporary Foreign Languages Studies, 9*, 22–27.

Li, S. (2013). Research and development in natural language processing. *Journal of Yanshan University (philosophy and Social Science Edition), 5*, 376–384.

Li, J., & Zhao, X. (2013). Research on recognition and application of corresponding word sequences in parallel texts. *Technology Enhanced Foreign Languages, 5*, 36–40.

Liu, Y. (1997). Machine translation is essentially a linguistic problem. *Applied Linguistics, 3*, 81–82.

Liu, Q. (2009). Recent advances in machine translation research. *Contemporary Linguistics, 2*, 147–158.

Miller, G. A., & Selfridge, J. A. (1950). Verbal context and the recall of meaningful material. *American Journal of Psychology, 63*, 176–185.

Pu, J. (2014). Corpus-driven translation research: Meaning units, translation units, and corresponding units. *Journal of PLA University of Foreign Languages, 1*, 53–63.

Teubert, W., & Čermáková, A. (2004). Directions in corpus linguistics. In M. A. K. Halliday et al. (Eds.), *Lexicology and corpus linguistics*. Continuum.

Wen, D. (2005). *Chinese lexicology*. The Commercial Press.

F. Hu, *An MT-Oriented Study of Corresponding Lexical Chunks in Business Correspondences from English to Chinese*,
https://doi.org/10.1007/978-981-99-4977-9

FSC
www.fsc.org
MIX
Papier aus verantwortungsvollen Quellen
Paper from responsible sources
FSC® C105338

If you have any concerns about our products,
you can contact us on
ProductSafety@springernature.com

In case Publisher is established outside the EU,
the EU authorized representative is:
Springer Nature Customer Service Center GmbH
Europaplatz 3, 69115 Heidelberg, Germany

Printed by Libri Plureos GmbH
in Hamburg, Germany